OVERSIZE FASHION KNITS

26 Cardigans and Pullovers Designed to Maximize Style and Ease

Frechverlag GmbH

STACKPOLE BOOKS

Guilford, Connecticut

Published by Stackpole Books
An imprint of The Rowman & Littlefield Publishing Group, Inc.
4501 Forbes Blvd., Ste. 200
Lanham, MD 20706
www.rowman.com

Distributed by NATIONAL BOOK NETWORK
800-462-6420

The original German edition was published as *Oversize Fashion*.
© 2015 frechverlag GmbH, 70499 Stuttgart, Germany (www.frech.de)
This edition is published by arrangement with Claudia Böhme Rights & Literary Agency, Hannover, Germany (www
.agency-boehme.com)

We would like to thank the Lana Grossa company for their support with this book: www.lanagrossa.com

Project Management and Editing: Miriam Heil
Photography: Frechverlag GmbH, 70499 Stuttgart, Germany; lichtpunkt, Michael Ruder, Stuttgart, Germany
Layout: Petra Theilfarth
Translation: Katharina Sokiran

British Library Cataloguing in Publication Information available

Library of Congress Cataloging-in-Publication Data
Names: Frechverlag GmbH.
Title: Oversize fashion knits : 26 cardigans and pullovers designed to maximize style and ease / Frechverlag GmbH.
Other titles: Oversize fashion. English
Description: First edition. | Lanham, MD : Stackpole Books, an imprint of The
Rowman & Littlefield Publishing Group, Inc., [2018] | Translation of the work originally in German: Oversize fashion.
Identifiers: LCCN 2018026780 | ISBN 9780811718394 (pbk. : alk. paper)
Subjects: LCSH: Knitting--Patterns. | Sweaters. | Women's clothing.
Classification: LCC TT825 .O9613 2018 | DDC 746.43/2041--dc23 LC record available at https://lccn.loc.gov/2018026780

♾™ The paper used in this publication meets the minimum requirements of American National Standard for Information
Sciences—Permanence of Paper for Printed Library Materials, ANSI/NISO Z39.48-1992.

First Edition

Printed in the United States of America

INTRODUCTION

Could there be anything better than cozying up in a big, soft, voluminous cardigan or sweater? If, on top of all that, it's also stylish and fashionable—that is truly the ultimate fashion knit bliss!

The magic word is "oversize," a worldwide runway trend. Over-proportioned sweaters, cardigans, and vests with relaxed fit are cozily warm and stylish eyecatchers at the same time. Whether in an easygoing boyfriend style or more feminine and intricate design, oversize is truly versatile and always captivating!

Thanks to three difficulty levels, the patterns in this book contain something for every skill set, from improving beginner to seasoned knitting pro. The majority of the projects are quick knits on large needles in bulky yarns, providing you with a new favorite piece in next to no time. We love oversize!

FASHION GOES GRAY

COLOR YOUR LIFE

FASHION GOES GRAY

CUDDLE UP

SUPERSOFT COZY CARDIGAN

STOCKINETTE STITCH

Knit on RS, purl on WS. Selvedge sts are worked in stockinette stitch, too.

ACCENTED DECREASES

At the beginning of the row, after having worked the first 2 sts, work sl1, k1, psso. Continue per instructions to the last 4 sts of the row, then knit the 3rd- and 4th-to-last sts together before working the last 2 sts.

ACCENTED INCREASES

At the beginning of the row, after the 2nd st, and at the end of the row, before the last 2 sts, make 1 from the bar between sts and knit this new st through the back loop.

>>> All pieces are worked with 3 strands of yarn held together, combining 2 strands of medium-weight yarn with 1 strand of light-weight yarn.

DIFFICULTY LEVEL 1

SIZES

Bust circumference for oversize fit: 36–38/40–42/44–46 in (91–97/102–107/112–117 cm)

Numbers for size 36–38 in (91–97 cm) are listed before the first slash, for 40–42 in (102–107 cm) between slashes, and for 44–46 in (112–117 cm) after the second slash. If only one number is given, it applies to all sizes.

MATERIALS

- #4 medium-weight yarn; shown in Lana Grossa Cool Wool Alpaca; 70% wool, 30% alpaca; 153 yd (140 m), 1.75 oz (50 g) per skein; #7 Light Gray, 12/13/14 skeins
- #3 light-weight mohair/silk yarn; shown in Lana Grossa Silkhair Melange; 70% mohair, 30% silk; 230 yd (210 m), 0.9 oz (25 g) per skein; #702 Light Gray/Light Beige mottled, 3/4/5 skeins
- US 11 (8 mm) and US 15 (10 mm) knitting needles
- US 13 (9 mm) circular knitting needle, 32 in (80 cm) long

GAUGE

In stockinette stitch on US 15 (10 mm) needles with 2 strands of #4 medium-weight yarn and 1 strand of #3 light-weight yarn held together, 10 sts and 15 rows = 4 x 4 in (10 x 10 cm)

(continued) CUDDLE UP

INSTRUCTIONS

BACK

With US 11 (8 mm) needles and holding 3 strands of yarn together as described, CO 54/58/62 sts. Work in stockinette stitch, beginning with a WS row in purl. When piece has reached a height of 2 in (5 cm) (9 rows) from cast-on row, mark both ends of the row with a piece of waste yarn or marker and change to US 15 (10 mm) needles.

For side shaping, in row 13 after the marked row, make an accented increase of 1 st each at the beginning and end of the row. Repeat the accented increase of 1 st each at both ends of the row twice more in every 10th row for a total of 60/64/68 sts. After 11/11¾/12½ in (28/30/32 cm) (42/46/48 rows) from the first marked spot, mark the beginning of the armhole at both ends of the row.

When armhole has reached a depth of 8¾/9/9½ in (22/23/24 cm) (32/34/36 rows), for shoulder sloping, at the beginning of the next 2 rows, BO 5/4/6 sts each, then BO 5/6/6 sts each the same way another 3 times. In the following row, place the remaining 20 back neckline sts for the collar on a stitch holder.

LEFT FRONT

With US 11 (8 mm) needles and holding 3 strands of yarn together as described, CO 47/49/51 sts. Work in stockinette stitch, beginning with a WS row in purl. When piece has reached a height of 2 in (5 cm) (9 rows) or the same number of rows you worked on the Back from cast-on row, mark the right edge of the piece and change to US 15 (10 mm) needles.

For side shaping at the right edge, in row 13 after the marked row, make an accented increase of 1 st, then make an accented increase of 1 st each twice more in every 10th row until you reach 50/52/54 sts. After 11/11¾/12½ in (28/30/32 cm) (42/46/48 rows) from first marked spot at the right edge, mark the beginning of the armhole.

When armhole has reached a depth of 8¾/9/9½ in (22/23/24 cm) (32/34/36 rows), bind off sts for shoulder sloping: 5/4/6 sts at the right edge, then BO 5/6/6 sts each the same way another 3 times. In the following row, place remaining 30 collar sts on a stitch holder.

RIGHT FRONT

With US 11 (8 mm) needles and holding 3 strands of yarn together as described, CO 47/49/51 sts. Work in stockinette stitch, beginning with a WS row in purl. When piece has reached a height of 2 in

(5 cm) (9 rows) from cast-on row, mark the left edge of the piece and change to US 15 (10 mm) needles.

For side shaping at the left edge, in row 13 after the marked row, make an accented increase of 1 st, then make an accented increase of 1 st each twice more in every 10th row until you reach 50/52/54 sts. After 11/11¾/12½ in (28/30/32 cm) (42/46/48 rows) from first marked spot at the left edge, mark the beginning of the armhole.

When armhole has reached a depth of 8¾/9/9½ in (22/23/24 cm) (32/34/36 rows), bind off sts for shoulder sloping: 5/4/6 sts at the left edge, then BO 5/6/6 sts each the same way another 3 times. In the following row, place remaining 30 collar sts on a stitch holder.

SLEEVES

Sew the Fronts and the Back together along the sloped shoulders.

With US 15 (10 mm) needles and 3 strands of yarn held together, pick up and knit 46/48/50 sts around each armhole edge between the marked spot and the beginning of the sloped section on the Back and Front. Work in stockinette stitch, beginning with a WS row in purl. At both ends of the row, for sleeve tapering, in the 10th/4th/8th row from beginning of sleeve, accent decrease 1 st each, then accent decrease 1 st each another 4/5/6 times in every 8th/8th/6th row, until you reach 36 sts. After 13¾ in (35 cm) (53 rows) from beginning of sleeve, change to US 11 (8 mm) needles

for sleeve cuff and continue in stockinette stitch. At 2 in (5 cm) sleeve cuff height, BO all sts.

Work the second sleeve the same way.

FINISHING

Wet block the pieces to indicated measurements and let dry. Sew side seams and sleeve seams.

Now, with US 13 (9 mm) circular needle and 3 strands of yarn held together, take up the collar sts (80 sts) from the holder and continue in stockinette stitch in back-and-forth rows. At 10 in (25 cm) collar width, BO all sts loosely.

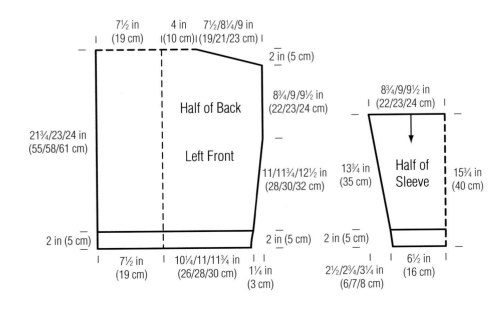

RIBBING

*P1, k1; repeat from *.

HALF BRIOCHE STITCH IN ROWS

Work in back-and-forth rows from Chart A. Stitches are shown as they appear from the RS of the fabric. Begin with the sts shown before the framed pattern repeat, repeat the pattern repeat, which is 2 sts wide, to the last 3 sts, and end with the sts shown after the framed pattern repeat. Work rows 1–3 only once, then repeat rows 2 and 3.

⟫⟫⟫ A stitch with a yarn over always counts as one stitch.

Chart A

Pattern repeat = 2 sts

● = 1 selvedge stitch

– = purl 1 on RS; knit 1 on WS

■ = knit 1 on RS; purl 1 on WS

⊖ = slip 1 stitch purlwise with yarn in front + 1 yarn over

Ⓤ = knit 1 yarn over together with the following stitch

HALF BRIOCHE STITCH IN ROUNDS

Work from Chart B, repeating rounds 1 and 2 of the pattern repeat. The pattern repeat is 2 sts wide.

Chart B

Pattern repeat = 2 sts

■ = knit 1 on RS; purl 1 on WS

⊖ = slip 1 stitch purlwise with yarn in front + 1 yarn over

Ⓤ = purl 1 yarn over together with the following stitch

CHOCOLATEBAR YUMMY LONG SWEATER

DIFFICULTY LEVEL 2

SIZES

Bust circumference for oversize fit: 36–40/42–46 in (91–102/107–117 cm)

Numbers for size 36–40 in (91–102 cm) are listed before the slash, for size 42–46 in (107–117 cm) after the slash. If only one number is given, it applies to both sizes.

MATERIALS

- #6 super-bulky-weight yarn; shown in Lana Grossa Yak Merino; 30% merino wool, 28% alpaca, 22% polyamide, 20% yak; 120 yd (110 m), 1.75 oz (50 g) per skein; #009 Gray Brown Mottled (A), #006 Black (B), and #012 Black Brown Mottled (C), 4/5 skeins each

- US 10 (6 mm) and US 11 (8 mm) knitting needles

- US 11 (8 mm) circular knitting needle, 24 in (60 cm) long

GAUGE

In half brioche stitch on US 11 (8 mm) needles, 11 sts and 22 rows = 4 x 4 in (10 x 10 cm)

INSTRUCTIONS

BACK

With US 10 (6 mm) needles and C, CO 63/69 sts. For the ribbing, work 3½ in (9 cm) (21 rows) in ribbing pattern, starting on a wrong side row with selv st, k1, and ending this row with k1, selv st.

Change to US 11 (8 mm) needles and continue in half brioche stitch. After 8 in (20 cm) (44 rows) from the ribbing, work another 8 in (20 cm) (44 rows) in B, then continue in A. After ¾/0 in (2/0 cm) (4/0 rows) from beginning of last color block, mark the beginning of the armhole at both ends of the row and continue to work even.

When armhole has reached a depth of 6¾/7½ in (17/19 cm) (38/42 rows), BO all sts as they appear (knit sts in knit and purl sts in purl) and mark the middle 25 sts for the neck opening.

(continued) CHOCOLATEBAR

FRONT

Work the same as the Back, but with rounded neckline. For this, at 4¾/5½ in (12/14 cm) (26/30 rows) armhole depth, BO the middle 11 sts and continue both parts separately. For further neckline shaping, at the inside (neck) edge, bind off sts as follows: at the beginning of every other row, 3 sts once, 2 sts once, and 1 st each twice. When armhole has reached a depth of 6¾/7½ in (17/19 cm) (38/42 rows), BO the remaining 19/22 shoulder sts in pattern.

Finish the other side the same way.

SLEEVES

Using US 10 (6 mm) needles and C, CO 27 sts. For the cuffs, work ribbing for 2½ in (6 cm) (15 rows), starting on a wrong side row with selv st, k1, and ending this row with k1, selv st.

Change to US 11 (8 mm) needles and continue in half brioche stitch, following stripe sequence. At both ends of the row, for sleeve shaping, in row 13 from cuff, inc 1 st each. Then in every 14th/10th row, inc 1 st each another 5/7 times (39/43 sts). Incorporate the new sts gained from the increases at both ends of the row into the half brioche stitch pattern. After 16½ in (42 cm) (94 rows) from the cuff, BO all sts loosely.

Work the second sleeve the same way.

FINISHING

Wet block all pieces to indicated measurements and let dry. Seam Back and Front at the sides from the bottom to the marked spot, and at the shoulders. Close sleeve seams.

With US 11 (8 mm) circular needle and A, pick up and knit 56 sts from the neckline edge and work for the turtleneck in half brioche stitch in rounds. When turtleneck is 8¼ in (21 cm) high, BO all sts loosely in pattern.

Sew the sleeves into the armholes.

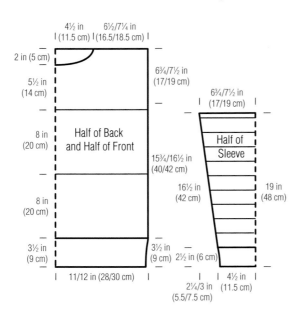

RIBBING
In RS rows, *k1, p2; repeat from *. In WS rows, work all sts as they appear (knit the knits and purl the purls).

INSTRUCTIONS

BACK

With US 7 (4.5 mm) needles, CO 161 sts. For bottom ribbing, work in ribbing pattern for 3¼ in (8 cm) (22 rows), starting the row with selv st, p1 and ending the row with p1, selv st. Change to US 8 (5 mm) needles and continue in ribbing.

First, to shape the curved sides, mark 91 sts in the center and work extended rows as follows: In the following RS row, turn 3 sts after the second one of the marked sts, make a yarn over onto the right needle and work back to the 3rd st after the first one of the marked sts. Turn again and make a yarn over onto the right needle. Incor-

STREETSTYLE LAID-BACK RIBBED SWEATER

DIFFICULTY LEVEL **3**

SIZES

Bust circumference in oversize fit: 36–44 in (91–112 cm)

Thanks to its relaxed shape, this garment will fit a range of sizes.

MATERIALS

- #4 medium-weight yarn; shown in Lana Grossa Alta Moda Superbaby Fine; 63% wool, 27% alpaca, 10% polyamide; 126 yd (115 m), .9 oz (25 g) per skein; #07 Raw White/Light Gray Mottled, 16 skeins
- US 7 (4.5 mm) and US 8 (5 mm) knitting needles
- US 8 (5 mm) circular knitting needle, 16 in (40 cm) long

GAUGE

In ribbing pattern on US 8 (5 mm) needles, 25 sts and 26 rows = 4 x 4 in (10 x 10 cm)

porate additional sts into the current row in this manner in every row at both ends of the row as follows: 3 more sts each, 9 times in all and the remaining 5 sts once, always turning with a yarn over and in the following extended row, either knitting or purling (staying in the ribbing pattern) the yarn over together with the following stitch, to avoid holes. When knitting or purling together, take care that the yarn overs end up on the WS of the work. This means for RS rows, at the left edge of the knitted piece, to knit or purl the yarn over together with the following stitch; for WS rows at the left edge, to knit or purl the yarn over together with the following stitch through the back loop.

(continued) STREETSTYLE

When all sts have been incorporated into the current row again, continue to add height to the sides by working even. After 14¼ in (36 cm) (94 rows) from the first full row, mark both ends of the row, and for armhole shaping, BO 1 st each. Then 24 times more in every other row, BO 1 st each (111 sts).

At armhole depth of 7½ in (19 cm) (50 rows), mark a second time. For shoulder sloping, at the beginning of the following RS and WS rows, BO 3 sts each, and in the same way 9 times more at both ends of the row, BO 3 sts each. After the last shoulder slope BO, place 51 center sts on a stitch holder for the collar.

FRONT

With US 7 (4.5 mm) needles, CO 116 sts. Work in ribbing pattern for 3¼ in (8 cm) (22 rows), starting the row with selv st, p1 and ending the row with p1, selv st.

Change to US 8 (5 mm) needles and continue in ribbing pattern. First, for the tails, work short rows at both ends of the row. The tail at the right edge is worked first. For this, in the following RS row, work 3 sts, turn, make a yarn over onto the right needle and work again to the end of the row. In every following RS row, incorporate 2 more sts each 15 times and either

knit or purl the yarn over from the previous row together with the following st, staying in pattern. Now, work a full row over all sts, then work the tip at the left edge in WS rows mirror inverted. For this, staying in ribbing pattern, either knit or purl the yarn over together with the following st through the back loop so that it always ends up on the wrong side. From here on, continue to work over all sts again.

In the 21st row from tip end, for center shaping, inc 2 sts (there will be 2 purl sts in the middle). *For this, from the bar between the two purl sts in the middle, make 1

knitwise twisted and make 1 purlwise. In WS rows, knit the knits and purl the purls, knit the 2 new sts in the middle. In the following 8th row, again make 1 knitwise twisted and make 1 purlwise from the bar between sts in the middle. Purl these sts in the following WS rows. In the following 8th row, again inc 2 sts purlwise as before (= first inc in center). Repeat these increases from * in every 8th row until you have increased a total of 14 times, 2 sts each.

AT THE SAME TIME, after 60 rows from the first full row, mark the beginning of armhole shaping

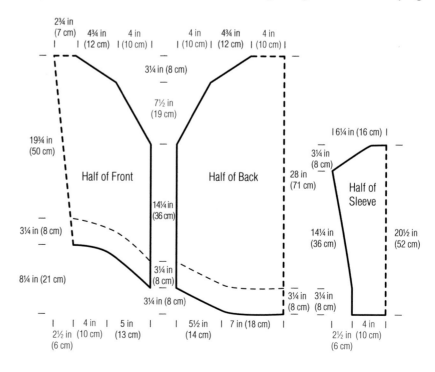

and, the same way as for the Back, at both ends of the row in every other row, BO 1 st each a total of 25 times. At armhole depth of 7½ in (19 cm) (50 rows), mark a second time. For shoulder sloping, at the beginning of the following RS and WS rows, BO 3 sts each and BO 3 sts each at both ends of the row 9 times more the same way. After the last increases and decreases, 34 sts remain on the needles; transfer these to a stitch holder for the collar.

SLEEVES

With US 7 (4.5 mm) needles, CO 52 sts. For the cuffs, work ribbing for ¾ in (2 cm) (6 rows), starting the first row 1 with selv st, p2 and working the last 3 sts of this row as p2, selv st. Change to US 8 (5 mm) needles and continue in ribbing. After 3¼ in (8 cm) (20 rows) from cast-on row, at both ends of the row, for sleeve shaping, inc 1 st each, then inc 1 st each in every 6th row for a total of 14 times (82 sts). Integrate the newly formed sts at both ends of the row into the ribbing pattern. After 14¼ in (36 cm) (94 rows) from the first increase, bind off sts for the sleeve cap at both ends of the row: at the beginning of the next 2 rows, BO 4 sts each, then at the beginning of every following row, BO 4 sts

each another 8 times and 5 sts each once. All sts have now been used up.

Work the second sleeve the same way.

FINISHING

Wet block pieces to indicated measurements and let dry.

Close side and shoulder seams to join Front and Back, taking care to leave armholes open between markers.

Transfer all formerly held 85 collar sts to US 8 (5 mm) circular needle and work ribbing in the round (in the center front, there should be 2 knit sts), continuing increases in the center front as established in the Front. At 6¼ in (16 cm) collar height, BO all sts loosely in pattern.

Close sleeve seams and sew sleeves into armholes.

RIBBING
*K2, p2; repeat from *.

STOCKINETTE STITCH
Knit on RS, purl on WS.

▶▶▶ The whole cardigan is worked with yarn held double.

INSTRUCTIONS

FRONTS AND BACK
Fronts and Back are worked sideways in one piece. With US 10.5/11 (7 mm) needles and yarn held double, CO 170/176 sts and work in stockinette stitch. After 12½/11¾ in (32/30 cm) (60/56 rows) from cast-on row, mark the beginning of the armhole at both ends of the row and continue to work even. After an additional 12½/14¼ in (32/36 cm) (60/68 rows) from the marked spot, mark the end of the armhole at both ends of the row and continue to work even. After 12½/11¾ in (32/30 cm) (60/56 rows) from the second marked spot, BO all sts loosely.

SALT 'N' PEPPER ELEGANT LONG CARDIGAN

DIFFICULTY LEVEL 1

SIZES
Bust circumference for oversize fit: 36–40/42–46 in (91–102/107–117 cm)

Numbers for size 36–40 in (91–102 cm) are listed before the slash, for size 42–46 in (107–117 cm) after the slash. If only one number is given, it applies to both sizes.

MATERIALS
- #4 medium-weight yarn; shown in Lana Grossa Garzato Nuovo; 37% merino wool, 33% polyamide, 20% mohair, 10% acrylic; 202 yd (185 m), 1.75 oz (50 g) per skein; #012 Black/Raw White/Silver, 12/13 skeins
- US 10.5/11 (7 mm) knitting needles
- US 10 (6 mm) circular knitting needle, 48 in (120 cm) long

GAUGE
In stockinette stitch on US 10.5/11 (7 mm) needles with two strands of yarn held together, 13 sts and 19 rows = 4 x 4 in (10 x 10 cm)

GARMENT SCHEMATIC PAGE 112

FINISHING AND SLEEVES
Wet block the piece to indicated measurements and let dry.

With yarn held double and US 10 (6 mm) needles, on both sides between the marked spots, pick up and knit 46/50 sts for the sleeves and work ribbing in back-and-forth rows, starting on a WS row with selv st, p1, and ending the row with p1, selv st. After 30 rows, reduce the stitch count to half by working either k2tog or p2tog across the next row. Continue in ribbing pattern to a sleeve length of 11½ in (29 cm) (54 rows), then BO all sts loosely in pattern, binding off the knits in knit and the purls in purl.

CHILL**OUT** *AIRY TUNIC*

SLIPPED SELVEDGE EDGING

Knit the first st in every row. Slip the last st in every row purlwise with yarn in front of work.

▶▶▶ Work all pieces with slipped selvedge edging.

RIBBING A

*K1, p1; repeat from *.

RIBBING B

Work from Chart A. Only RS rows are shown; in WS rows, work all sts as they appear. Begin with the sts shown before the framed pattern repeat, repeat the pattern repeat, which is 2 sts wide, to the last 3 sts, and end with the sts shown after the framed pattern repeat. Work rows 1–4 once.

Chart A

| ● | ■ | – | ■ | – | ■ | ● | 3 |

● = 1 selvedge stitch
– = purl 1
■ = knit 1

Pattern repeat = 2 sts

FISHERMAN'S RIB

Work in back-and-forth rows from Charts B and C. Stitches are shown as they are worked. Begin with the sts shown before the framed pattern repeat, repeat the pattern repeat, which is 2 sts wide, to the last 3 sts, and end with the sts shown after the framed pattern repeat.

▶▶▶ A stitch with a yarn over counts as one stitch.

First, work one height-wise pattern repeat of rows 1–4 from Chart

B, then repeat only rows 3 and 4 of Chart B another 6 times (16 rows), then work rows 1–4 of Chart C once, then repeat only rows 3 and 4 of Chart C.

▶▶▶ When transitioning from Chart B to Chart C, owing to the staggered stitch pattern, in two consecutive rows, the st with yo will be slipped as shown.

Chart B

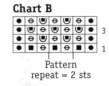

● = 1 selvedge stitch
⊖ = slip 1 stitch with yarn in front + 1 yarn over
Ʊ = knit 1 yarn over together with the following stitch
■ = knit 1

Chart C

Pattern repeat = 2 sts

ACCENTED DECREASES A

Start the row with selv st, k3tog, work the last 4 sts of the row as slip 1 knitwise, k2tog, pass the slipped st over, selv st. At both ends of the row, 2 sts each are decreased.

DIFFICULTY LEVEL 2

SIZES

Bust circumference in oversize fit: 36–42 in (91–107 cm)

Thanks to its relaxed shape, this garment will fit a range of sizes.

MATERIALS

- #5 bulky-weight yarn; shown in Lana Grossa Cashsilk Metal; 40% polyamide, 30% bamboo, 15% silk, 15% cashmere; 82 yd (75 m), 1.75 oz (50 g) per skein; #309 White/Silver, 12 skeins
- US 11 (8 mm) knitting needles
- US 11 (8 mm) circular knitting needle, 24 in (60 cm) long

GAUGE

In fisherman's rib on US 11 (8 mm) needles, 12 sts and 32 rows = 4 x 4 in (10 x 10 cm)

ACCENTED DECREASES B

At the beginning of the row, work the first 7 sts as selv st, 3 sts in fisherman's rib, k3tog; at the end of the row, work to the last 7 sts, ending the row with slip 1 knitwise, k2tog, pass the slipped st over, 3 sts in fisherman's rib, selv st. At both ends of the row, 2 sts each are decreased.

INSTRUCTIONS

BACK

Cast on 79 sts. For bottom ribbing, work ¾ in (2 cm) (4 rows) in ribbing pattern B according to Chart A. Continue in fisherman's rib as described.

After 11 in (28 cm) (90 rows) from end of bottom ribbing, mark the beginning of the armhole at both ends of the row and continue to work even. For shoulder sloping, at armhole depth of 7½ in (19 cm) (62 rows), at the beginning of the next 2 rows, BO 1 st each, then at both ends of the row in every other row, work Accented Decrease A, decreasing 2 sts each for a total of 13 times, and, finally, BO 2 sts once.

AT THE SAME TIME as the 11th shoulder decrease, for back neckline, BO 21 middle sts on the Back, then continue both parts separately. After the last shoulder slope BO, the sts on one side have been used up.

Finish the other side the same way.

FRONT

Work the same as the Back, but with V-neckline. For this, after only 10½ in (27 cm) (88 rows) from end of bottom ribbing, BO the center st and continue both parts separately. At inside edge, for the sloped neckline, in every 16th row, work Accented Decrease B to dec 2 sts a total of 5 times. For shoulder sloping, at armhole depth of 7½ in (19 cm) (62 rows), at both ends of the row, BO 1 st each, then in every other row, work Accented Decrease A, decreasing 2 sts each for a total of 13 times, and finally, BO 2 sts once.

FINISHING

Wet block pieces to indicated measurements and let dry.

Sew Front and Back together at the shoulders and sides, leaving the armholes open. Using circular needle, pick up and knit 90 sts around the neckline edge. Work the neckband in ribbing pattern A in the round, making sure a knit st ends up in the center front. For the point, in every other round, slip the center st together with the st before it knitwise, knit the next st and pass the slipped sts over. When neckband has reached 1¼ in (3 cm), BO all sts in pattern, knit sts in knit and purl sts in purl.

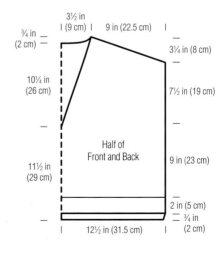

¾ in (2 cm)
3½ in (9 cm)
9 in (22.5 cm)
3¼ in (8 cm)
10¼ in (26 cm)
7½ in (19 cm)
Half of Front and Back
9 in (23 cm)
11½ in (29 cm)
2 in (5 cm)
¾ in (2 cm)
12½ in (31.5 cm)

GARTER STITCH SELVEDGE

Slip the first st of every row knitwise. Knit the last st of every row.

》》》 Work all parts with garter stitch selvedge.

RIBBING

*K2, p2; repeat from *.

GARTER STITCH

In rows: knit on RS, knit on WS.

INSTRUCTIONS

BACK WITH SLEEVES

First, the piece is worked sideways without the bottom ribbing, starting from the sleeve. Cast on 20 sts using US 10.5/11 (7 mm) needles and work garter stitch for 3 rows.

Before row 4, change to US 11 (8 mm) needles and in this row, inc 14 sts evenly distributed, as follows: k3, *m1, k1, rep from * 13 times more, k3 (34 sts total).

At 4 in (10 cm) (22 rows) from cast-on row, at the left edge of the knitted piece, for the side extension, CO an additional 36 sts (70 sts total). Change to US 11 (8 mm) circular needle and continue in garter stitch over all sts. After 19/20½ in (48/52 cm) (106/114 rows)

BLACKVELVET FAVORITE GARTER STITCH DRESS

DIFFICULTY LEVEL 1

SIZES

Bust circumference for oversize fit: 36–38/40–42 in (91–97/102–107 cm)

Numbers for size 36–38 in (91–97 cm) are listed before the slash, for size 40–42 in (102–107 cm) after the slash. If only one number is given, it applies to both sizes.

MATERIALS

- #5 bulky-weight yarn; shown in Lana Grossa Mille II; 50% merino wool, 50% acrylic; 61 yd (55 m), 1.75 oz/50 g per skein; #015 Black, 13/14 skeins
- US 10.5/11 (7 mm) and US 11 (8 mm) knitting needles
- US 10.5/11 (7 mm) and US 11 (8 mm) circular knitting needles, 32 in (80 cm) long

GAUGE

In garter stitch on US 11 (8 mm) needles, 11 sts and 22 rows = 4 x 4 in (10 x 10 cm)

(continued) **BLACK**VELVET

from the cast-on row extension, BO 36 sts at the left edge of the knitted piece.

For the second sleeve, first continue to work even over the remaining 34 sts. When sleeve has reached 3¼ in (8 cm) (18 rows), dec 14 sts evenly distributed, as follows: k3, *k2tog, rep from * 13 times more, k3 (20 sts total), and continue with US 10.5/11 (7 mm) needles in garter stitch. At total sleeve length of 4 in (10 cm) (22 rows), BO all sts.

FRONT WITH SLEEVES

Work the same as the Back.

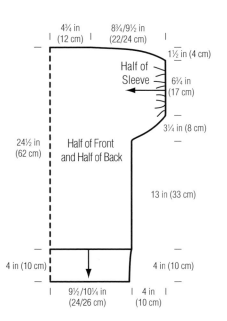

FINISHING

Wet block pieces to indicated measurements and let dry.

Sew Front and Back together at the tops of the sleeves and shoulders over 8¾/9½ in (22/24 cm) from both outside edges. In between, leave 9½ in (24 cm) open for the neckline. Now, seam the bottom edges of the sleeves and close the side seams.

Using US 10.5/11 (7 mm) circular needle, pick up and knit 114/118 sts along the bottom edge and join to work in the round. Work the tall bottom ribbing in ribbing pattern in the round, decreasing 10 sts evenly distributed in round 1 by k2/4, *k2tog, k9, rep from * 9 times more, k2/4 (104/108 total sts). When bottom edge has reached 4 in (10 cm), BO all sts loosely in pattern, binding off the knits in knit and the purls in purl.

>>> Arrows in the schematic indicate the knitting direction.

MARBLESTRIPES

FASHIONABLE KIMONO COAT

GARTER STITCH SELVEDGE

Slip the first st of every row knitwise. Knit the last st of every row.

>>> Work all parts with garter stitch selvedge.

RIBBING

*K1, p1; repeat from *.

REVERSE STOCKINETTE STITCH

Purl on RS, knit on WS.

STOCKINETTE STITCH

Knit on RS, purl on WS.

ACCENTED DECREASES

At the beginning of the row, after the first two sts, p2tog. At the end of the row, work to last 4 sts of row, then slip1, p1, psso (slip 1 knitwise, purl the next st and pass the slipped st over), work last 2 sts.

INSTRUCTIONS

BACK WITH TWO SLEEVE HALVES

Using US 10.5/11 (7 mm) needles, CO 66/72/78 sts. For bottom ribbing, work 1¼ in (3 cm) (6 rows) in ribbing pattern. Continue in reverse stockinette.

DIFFICULTY LEVEL 2

SIZES

Bust circumference for oversize fit: 36–38/40–42/44–46 in (91–97/102–107/112–117 cm)

Numbers for size 36–38 in (91–97 cm) are listed before the first slash, for 40–42 in (102–107 cm) between slashes, and for 44–46 in (112–117 cm) after the second slash. If only one number is given, it applies to all sizes.

MATERIALS

- #5 bulky-weight yarn; shown in Lana Grossa Medio; 53% wool, 47% acrylic; 98.5 yd (90 m), 1.75 oz (50 g) per skein; #029 Gray/Graphite/White/Anthracite/Light Gray, 14/15/16 skeins
- US 10.5/11 (7 mm) knitting needles
- US 10.5/11 (7 mm) circular knitting needles, 32 in (80 cm) and 48 in (120 cm) long

GAUGE

In reverse stockinette stitch with US 10.5/11 (7 mm) needles, 12.5 sts and 21 rows = 4 x 4 in (10 x 10 cm)

(continued) MARBLESTRIPES

Work side and sleeve increases at beginning and end of row, starting in the 7th row from the end of the bottom ribbing, by increasing 1 st at each end by making 1 between sts purlwise twisted, then repeating increases in every 8th row, 5 times total; in every 6th row, 8 times total; and in every other row, 3 times total. Now, cast on additional sts at the outside edges: for the right edge, at the beginning of a RS row; for the left edge, at the beginning of a WS row, as follows: 2 sts, 3 times in all; 3 sts, once; 4 sts, once; 5 sts, once; 6 sts, once;

and 7 sts, once (162/168/174 sts). To accommodate all sts, change to circular needle with longer cord as stitch count increases.

Continue to work even for sleeves. After 5/5½/6 in (13/14/15 cm) (28/30/32 rows) from last sleeve increase, bind off sts at both ends of the row for shoulder sloping at sleeves as follows: at the beginning of the next 2 rows, BO 3 sts each, then BO 3 sts each the same way 14/15/16 times more, BO 2 sts each once, BO 5 sts each once, and BO 4 sts each a total of 5 times.

AT THE SAME TIME as the third-to-last shoulder decrease, BO the middle 10 sts for the round neckline, and continue both parts separately.

For further neckline shaping, at the inside (neck) edge, BO 2 sts each twice more at the beginning of every other row. After the last shoulder decrease, the sts on one side have been used up. Work the other half the same way, but mirror inverted.

LEFT FRONT WITH HALF A SLEEVE

Using US 10.5/11 (7 mm) needles, CO 34/37/40 sts. For bottom ribbing, work 1¼ in (3 cm) (6 rows) in ribbing pattern. Continue in reverse stockinette.

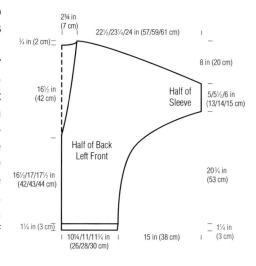

At the right edge, work side and sleeve increases, starting in the 7th row from the end of the bottom ribbing, by increasing 1 st each by making 1 between sts purlwise twisted, then repeating increases in every 8th row, 5 times total; in every 6th row, 8 times total; and in every other row, 3 times total.

Now, cast on additional sts at the right edge: 2 sts, 3 times in all; 3 sts, once; 4 sts, once; 5 sts, once; 6 sts, once; and 7 sts, once (82/85/88 sts). To accommodate all sts, change to circular needle with longer cord as stitch count increases.

After 16½/17/17½ in (42/43/44 cm) (88/90/92 rows) from end of bottom ribbing, at the left edge, for neckline shaping, accent decrease 1 st, repeating this accented decrease of 1 st in every 10th row a total of 9 times.

AT THE SAME TIME, after 5/5½/6 in (13/14/15 cm) (28/30/32 rows) from last sleeve increase, at the right edge, for shoulder sloping at sleeves, bind off sts as follows: BO 3 sts once, BO 3 sts 14/15/16 times more, BO 2 sts once, BO 5 sts once, and BO 4 sts a total of 5 times. After the last decrease, all sts have been used up.

RIGHT FRONT WITH HALF A SLEEVE

Using US 10/11.5 (7 mm) needles, CO 34/37/40 sts. For bottom rib-bing, work 1¼ in (3 cm) (6 rows) in ribbing pattern. Continue in reverse stockinette.

At the left edge, work side and sleeve increases, starting in the 7th row from the end of the bottom ribbing, by increasing 1 st each by making 1 between sts purlwise twisted, then repeating increases in every 8th row, 5 times total; in every 6th row, 8 times total; and in every other row, 3 times total.

Now, cast on additional sts at the left edge: 2 sts, 3 times in all; 3 sts, once; 4 sts, once; 5 sts, once; 6 sts, once; and 7 sts, once (82/85/88 sts). To accommodate all sts, change to circular needle with longer cord as stitch count increases.

After 16½/17/17½ in (42/43/44 cm) (88/90/92 rows) from end of bottom ribbing, at right edge, for neckline shaping, make an accented decrease of 1 st, repeating this accented decrease of 1 st in every 10th row for a total of 9 times.

AT THE SAME TIME, after 5/5½/6 in (13/14/15 cm) (28/30/32 rows) from last sleeve increase, at the left edge, for shoulder sloping at sleeves, BO 3 sts once, BO 3 sts 14/15/16 times more, BO 2 sts once, BO 5 sts once, and BO 4 sts a total of 5 times. After the last decrease, all sts have been used up.

FINISHING

Wet block pieces to indicated measurements and let dry.

Sew Fronts and Back together at the shoulders, sleeves, and sides.

Now, using long circular needle, pick up and knit 197/201/205 sts from the vertical front edges and along the whole neckline edge. For the front band, work stockinette stitch in rows, beginning with a WS row in purl. At front band width of 2¾ in (7 cm), BO loosely in knit.

COLOR YOUR LIFE

BLUESKIES

FEATHERWEIGHT SEQUINED CARDIGAN

RIBBING
*K2, p2; repeat from *.

STOCKINETTE STITCH
Knit on RS, purl on WS.

EXTENDED ROWS
Here, you will not work all the sts in the row. Stop before the sts that will stay on the needle are worked. Now, make a yarn over onto the right needle and tighten, turn and work back in the other direction on the other side. In the following extended row, staying in pattern, either knit or purl the yarn over together with the following st twisted to avoid holes.

ACCENTED DECREASES
At the beginning of the row, after the first two sts, k2tog. At the end of the row, work the last 4 sts as follows: sl1, k1, psso, work last 2 sts. This way, you dec 1 st each at both ends of the row.

INSTRUCTIONS

LEFT FRONT
With US 9 (5.5 mm) needles and yarn held single, CO 46/50 sts. For bottom ribbing, work 1½ in (4 cm) (9 rows) in ribbing pattern, starting on a WS row with selv st, p1, and ending the row with p1, selv st. Now, continue with US 9 (5.5 mm) needles and yarn held single, working in stockinette stitch. For A-line shaping, work accented decreases at the right edge *only* as follows: in the 5th row from bottom ribbing, accent decrease 1 st, then repeat accent decrease of 1 st each in every 10th row, 9 times more; in every 8th row, 6 times more; and, finally, in every 6th row, 6 times more (24/28 sts).

DIFFICULTY LEVEL 2

SIZES
Bust circumference for oversize fit: 36–40/42–46 in (91–102/107–117 cm)

Numbers for size 36–40 in (91–97 cm) are listed before the slash, for size 42–46 in (107–117 cm) after the slash. If only one number is given, it applies to both sizes.

MATERIALS
- #4 medium-weight yarn; shown in Lana Grossa Lace Paillettes; 45% alpaca, 20% wool, 15% polyamide, 5% polyester; 164 yd (150 m), 0.9 oz (25 g) per skein; #10 Dark Blue, 8/9 skeins
- US 9 (5.5 mm) and US 10 (6 mm) knitting needles
- US 10 (6 mm) circular knitting needles, 24 in (60 cm) and 48 in (120 cm) long
- Button, 1 in (28 mm)

GAUGE
In stockinette stitch on US 9 (5.5 mm) needles with yarn held single, 17 sts and 26 rows = 4 x 4 in (10 x 10 cm)

In ribbing pattern on US 10 (6 mm) needles with yarn held double, 14 sts and 12 rows (measured stretched) = 4 x 2 in (10 x 5 cm)

For neckline shaping, after 17½ in (44 cm) (114 rows) from bottom ribbing, at the left edge, accent decrease 1 st, then repeat accent decrease of 1 st each in every 6th row, 2 times more, and in every 8th row, 2 times more (19/23 sts).

After 28¼ in (71.5 cm) (180 rows) from bottom ribbing, at the right edge, bind off sts for shoulder sloping, as follows: BO 5/6 sts once; then in every 3rd row, BO 5/6 sts each; and, finally, BO 4/5 sts once. All sts have now been used up.

RIGHT FRONT

With US 9 (5.5 mm) needles and yarn held single, CO 46/50 sts. For bottom ribbing, work 1½ in (4 cm) (9 rows) in ribbing pattern, starting on a WS row with selv st, p1, and ending the row with p1, selv st. Now, with US 9 (5.5 mm) needles and yarn held single, continue in stockinette stitch.

For A-line shaping, work accented decreases at the left edge *only*, as follows: in the 5th row from bottom ribbing, accent

decrease 1 st, then repeat accent decrease of 1 st each in every 10th row, 9 times more; in every 8th row, 6 times more; and, finally, in every 6th row, 6 times more (24/28 sts).

For neckline shaping, after 17½ in (44 cm) (114 rows) from bottom ribbing, at the right edge only, accent decrease 1 st, then repeat accent decrease of 1 st each in every 6th row, 2 times more; and in every 8th row, 2 times more (19/23 sts).

After 28¼ in (71.5 cm) (180 rows) from bottom ribbing, at the left edge, bind off sts for shoulder sloping, as follows: BO 5/6 sts once; then in every 3rd row, BO 5/6 sts each; and finally, BO 4/5 sts once. All sts have now been used up.

BACK WITH SLEEVES

▶▶▶ The Back is worked sideways in one piece from sleeve to sleeve. The sleeves are formed while seaming up.

Start with the left sleeve and, with US 10 (6 mm) needles and yarn held double, CO 106 sts. For the bottom ribbing, work in ribbing pattern for 2½ in (6 cm) (13 rows), starting on a WS row with selv st, p1, and ending the row with p1, selv st.

Now, with US 9 (5.5 mm) needles and yarn held single, continue in stockinette stitch, increasing in the first row as follows: *k5, m1 from the bar between sts and knit it tbl, repeat from * 21 times more; after the last increase, k1 (128 sts).

At 12½ in (31.5 cm) (82 rows) from bottom ribbing, work extended rows for A-shaping on the Back. For this, at the right edge of the work, in the next row, work 8 sts, make a yarn over onto the needle, turn and work back on the other side; then in every other row, incorporate 8 more sts into the current row each time, 14 times in all, always knitting the yarn overs together with the following st. From here on, continue to work over all sts again and, AT THE SAME TIME, for shoulder sloping, at the

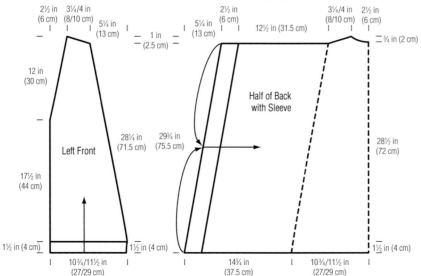

(continued) BLUE SKIES

left edge of the knitted piece, inc 1 st by kfb into the selv st, then inc 1 st each in every 6th row another 3 times (132 sts).

When shoulder width has reached 3/4 in (8/10 cm), at the left edge of the knitted piece, bind off for the neckline, as follows: BO 2 sts once; then in the 2nd row, BO 1 st once (129 sts). At 2½ in (6 cm) neckline width, the center back of the neckline has been reached.

For the other side of the neckline, at the left edge of the knitted piece, in the 2nd row, now CO 1 st again once, then in the following 2nd row, CO another 2 new sts (132 sts). For shoulder sloping, at the left edge of the knitted piece,

BO 1 st each in every 6th row, 4 times in all (128 sts).

Now, work extended rows again. For this, at the left edge of the knitted piece, at the beginning of the row, leave 16 sts unworked on the needle, make a yarn over and turn work, then in every other row, leave 8 sts unworked, 15 times in all. After this, resume to work over all sts again. Measured from the first full row, work another 12½ in (31.5 cm) (82 rows) even in stockinette stitch. In the following row: *k4, k2tog, rep from * 21 times more; after the last decrease, k1 (106 sts). Change to US 10 (6 mm) needles and, with yarn held double, work in ribbing pattern

for 2½ in (6 cm) (13 rows) for the ribbed edging. After the last row of ribbed edging, BO all sts in pattern: knit sts in knit and purl sts in purl.

FINISHING

Wet block pieces to indicated measurements and let dry.

Sew the Fronts to the Back along the sloped shoulders. For the sleeves, fold the sides of the Back over toward the top and bottom with overlapping ribbed edging according to schematic and arrows shown in schematic, then sew on.

Now, with US 10 (6 mm) circular needle and yarn held double, for button band and neckline edging, pick up and knit a total of 232 sts along the vertical edges of the Fronts, the sloped part of the neckline, and the back neckline. For the edging, work ribbing in back-and-forth rows, starting on a WS row with selv st, p2, and working the last 3 sts of the row as p2, selv st. When edging has reached 1¼ in (3 cm), work buttonholes as follows: on the Right Front, at the beginning of the sloped part of the neckline, BO 2 sts and in the following row, CO 2 sts again. When edging has reached 2½ in (6 cm), BO sts very loosely in pattern. Sew on the button.

》》》 Arrows in the schematic indicate the knitting direction.

REDPEPPER
FEMININE MOSS STITCH SWEATER

RIBBING
*K1, p1; repeat from *.

MOSS STITCH
Row 1 (RS): Selv st, *k1, p1, repeat from * to last st, selv st.

Rows 2 and 4: Work the sts between selv sts as they appear: knit the knits and purl the purls.
Row 3: Selv st, *p1, k1, repeat from * to last st, selv st.
Repeat rows 1–4.

DIFFICULTY LEVEL 1

SIZES
Bust circumference for oversize fit: 36–38/40–42/44–46 in (91–97/102–107/112–117 cm)

Numbers for size 36–38 in (91–97 cm) are listed before the first slash, for 40–42 in (102–107 cm) between slashes, and for 44–46 in (112–117 cm) after the second slash. If only one number is given, it applies to all sizes.

MATERIALS
- #6 super-bulky-weight yarn; shown in Lana Grossa Alta Moda Superbaby; 67% merino wool, 30% alpaca, 3% polyamide; 66 yd (60 m), 1.75 oz (50 g) per skein; #021 Red-purple, 14/15/16 skeins
- US 13 (9 mm) and US 17 (12 mm) knitting needles

GAUGE
In moss stitch on US 17 (12 mm) needles, 9 sts and 14 rows = 4 x 4 in (10 x 10 cm)

In ribbing pattern on US 13 (9 mm) needles, 14 sts and 18 rows = 4 x 4 in (10 x 0 cm)

INSTRUCTIONS

BACK

Using US 13 (9 mm) needles, CO 54 sts. For the wide bottom ribbing, work in ribbing pattern for 5 in (13 cm) (25 rows), starting with a WS row. Change to US 17 (12 mm) needles and continue in moss stitch.

After 19/18/17¼ in (48/46/44 cm) (68/64/62 rows) from bottom ribbing, mark the beginning of the armhole at both ends of the row. When armhole has reached a depth of 6¼/7/8 in (16/18/20 cm) (22/26/28 rows), BO all sts.

FRONT

Work the same as the Back. Close the shoulder seams.

SLEEVES

Using US 13 (9 mm) needles, pick up a total of 36/42/48 sts to both sides of the shoulder seam between the marked spots and work in ribbing pattern, starting on a WS row with p1. For sleeve tapering, BO at both ends of the row as follows: in row 40, BO 1 st each once; then in every 20th row, BO 1 st each, 3 times; and in every 16th row, BO 1 st each, 4 times (34/36/40 sts). At sleeve length of 18½ in (47 cm) (85 rows), BO remaining sts.

Work the second sleeve the same way.

FINISHING

Wet block pieces to indicated measurements and let dry.

Sew side seams and sleeve seams.

》》》 The arrow in the schematic indicates the knitting direction.

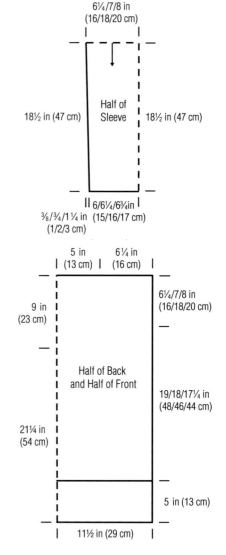

GARTER STITCH SELVEDGE

Knit the selv sts in both RS and WS rows.

GARTER STITCH

In rows: knit on RS, knit on WS.
In rounds: alternate 1 knit round and 1 purl round.

BASKET WEAVE PATTERN

Work from chart in rows or rounds. Shown are only the RS rows, or odd-numbered rounds; in WS rows and even-numbered rounds, knit the knits and purl the purls. Work the pattern repeat (12 sts wide) once, repeating rows/rounds 1–4.

pattern repeat = 12 sts

= hold 2 sts on cable needle behind work, knit 1, then knit 2 from cable needle

= hold 1 st on cable needle in front of work, knit 2, then knit 1 from cable needle

= knit 1

》》》 Work all parts with garter stitch selvedge, tightening the working yarn at the selvedge stitch.

INDIAN**CURRY** CLEVER CURRY-COLORED CABLED SWEATER

DIFFICULTY LEVEL 2

SIZES

Bust circumference for oversize fit: 36–38/40–42 in (91–102/107–117 cm)

Numbers for size 36–38 in (91–96 cm) are listed before the slash, for size 40–42 in (101–107 cm) after the slash. If only one number is given, it applies to both sizes.

MATERIALS

- #5 bulky-weight yarn; shown in Lana Grossa Mille II; 50% merino wool, 50% acrylic; 61 yd (55 m), 1.75 oz (50 g) per skein; #46 Curry, 18/19 skeins
- US 11 (8 mm) knitting needles
- US 11 (8 mm) circular knitting needle, 24 in (60 cm) long

GAUGE

In garter stitch on US 11 (8 mm) needles, 11 sts and 22 rows = 4 x 4 in (10 x 10 cm)

In basket weave pattern on US 11 (8 mm) needles, 12 sts = 3¼ in (8 cm)

INSTRUCTIONS

BACK

Cast on 58/64 sts and work 1 WS row in knit. Now, continue in the following pattern: selv st, work 22/25 sts in garter stitch, work 12 sts in basket weave pattern, work 22/25 sts in garter stitch, selv st.

After 14½ in (37 cm) (81 rows) from cast-on row, mark the beginning of the armhole at both ends of the row and continue to work even. When armhole has reached a depth of 6¾/7 in (17/18 cm) (38/40 rows), place all shoulder and neckline sts on a stitch holder.

FRONT

Work the same as the Back.

SLEEVES

Cast on 38 sts and work 1 WS row in knit. Now, continue in the fol-lowing pattern: selv st, 12 sts garter stitch, 12 sts in basket weave pattern, 12 sts garter stitch, selv st. For side shaping, at both ends of the row, inc 1 st each from the bar between sts in rows 36 and 72/rows 26, 52, and 78, and knit the new sts tbl (42/44 sts). After 19¼ in (49 cm) (107 rows) from cast-on row, BO all sts loosely.

Work the second sleeve the same way.

FINISHING

Wet block pieces to indicated measurements and let dry.

Sew Back and Front together at the sides from the bottom to the marked spot. Place the formerly held sts of the Back and Front (116/128 sts) on a US 11 (8 mm) circular needle.

For shoulders and collar, continue the stitch pattern in the established rhythm. In the first round, ssk or k2tog the selv sts of all pieces with the preceding or following st (112/124 sts). Mark these two spots for shoulder seam placement. For shoulder sloping, in the next knit round, at both ends of the row, k2tog the 2 sts before the 1st and 3rd shoulder seam line and ssk the 2 sts after the 2nd and 4th shoulder seam line. This way, 4 sts will be decreased in every round. Repeat these decreases in every other round 9 times more/12 times more (72 sts), then work even for the collar. After 10½ in (27 cm) (60 rnds) from the beginning of the shoulders, BO all sts loosely. Close sleeve seams and sew sleeves into armholes slightly stretched.

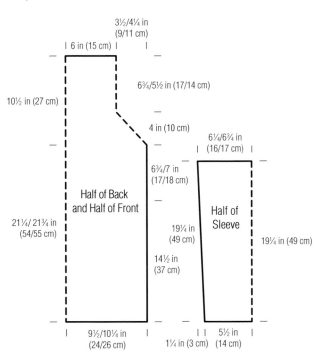

RIBBING
*K1, p1; repeat from *.

HALF BRIOCHE STITCH
Worked over an odd number of sts.

Row 1 (WS): Selv st, *slip next st purlwise with yarn in front and make a yarn over, k1, repeat from * to last 2 sts, slip st purlwise with yarn in front and make a yarn over, selv st.

Row 2 (RS): Selv st, *knit the yarn over together with the slipped st of the previous row, p1, repeat from * to last 3 sts, knit the yarn over together with the slipped st of the previous row, selv st.

Repeat rows 1 and 2.

INSTRUCTIONS

BACK
Using US 9 (5.5 mm) needles, CO 93/101/107 sts and work in half brioche stitch. After 18 in (45.5 cm) (109 rows) from cast-on row, work 3 sts, mark 7 sts for first bias band, work to last 10 sts, mark 7 sts for second bias band, work last 3 sts.

DEEPSEA CLASSIC CARDIGAN IN SEA GREEN

DIFFICULTY LEVEL 2

SIZES
Bust circumference for oversize fit: 36–38/40–42/44–46 in (91–97/102–107/112–117 cm)

Numbers for size 36–38 in (91–97 cm) are listed before the first slash, for 40–42 in (102–107 cm) between slashes, and for 44–46 in (112–117 cm) after the second slash. If only one number is given, it applies to all sizes.

MATERIALS
- #4 medium-weight yarn; shown in Lana Grossa Garzato Fleece; 70% alpaca, 30% polyamide; 246 yd (225 m), 1.75 oz (50 g) per skein; #15 Turquoise/Black, 5/6/7 skeins
- US 9 (5.5 mm) knitting needles
- US 9 (5.5 mm) circular knitting needle, 24 in (60 cm) long
- 3 buttons, 1¼ in (3 cm)

GAUGE
In half brioche stitch on US 9 (5.5 mm) needles, 17 sts and 24 rows = 4 x 4 in (10 x 10 cm)

(continued) DEEPSEA

sloping, BO remaining 55/55/57 sts; the outermost 4/4/5 sts are still part of the shoulder sloping, the middle 47 sts belong to the neckline. Mark the neckline accordingly.

LEFT FRONT

Using US 9 (5.5 mm) needles, CO 43/47/51 sts and work in half brioche stitch. After 8¾ in (22 cm) (53 rows) from cast-on row, for pocket slit, work 9/11/13 sts, BO the middle 25 sts and work 9/11/13 sts. Place the sts on a stitch holder.

For the pocket lining, using US 9 (5.5 mm) needles, CO 25 sts and work 5 in (13 cm) (31 rows) in half brioche stitch. Now, incorporate the 25 pocket lining sts in place of the bound-off sts into the current row and continue working over all 43/47/51 sts.

After 15½ in (39 cm) (93 rows) from cast-on row, for neckline shaping, bind off sts at the left edge: 1 st once, and in every other row 1 st, a total of 19 times.

After 18 in (45.5 cm) (109 rows) from cast-on row, work 3 sts and mark 7 sts for bias band. In the following RS row, and in every other row thereafter, before the bias band, inc 1 st from the bar between sts in pattern and p2tog the 2 sts after the bias band. When the bias band has traveled all the

way to the left edge, continue working neckline decreases over the last 2 sts, at the same time continuing increases.

At 26½ in (67 cm) (161 rows) from cast-on row, for shoulder sloping, at the right edge, BO 3/5/5 sts once; and then in every other row, BO 4 sts, 5 times/5 sts, twice; and BO 4 sts, 3 times/5 sts, 5 times.

RIGHT FRONT

Using US 9 (5.5 mm) needles, CO 43/47/51 sts and work in half brioche stitch. After 8¾ in (22 cm) (53 rows) from cast-on row for pocket slit, work 9/11/13 sts, BO the middle 25 sts, and work 9/11/13 sts. Place the sts on a stitch holder.

For the pocket lining, using US 9 (5.5 mm) needles, CO 25 sts and work 5 in (13 cm) (31 rows) in half brioche stitch. Now, incorporate the 25 pocket lining sts in place of the bound-off sts into the current row and continue working over all 43/47/51 sts.

After 15½ in (39 cm) (93 rows) from cast-on row for neckline shaping, at the right edge, BO 1 st once, and in every other row 1 st, a total of 19 times.

After 18 in (45.5 cm) (109 rows) from cast-on row, work to last 10 sts of row, mark 7 sts for bias band and work 3 sts. In the following

In the following RS row, and in every other row thereafter, before the first bias band, inc 1 st from the bar between sts in pattern (either purlwise tbl or knitwise tbl) and after the first bias band, p2tog next 2 sts. At the end of the row, before the second bias band, p2tog, and after the second bias band, inc 1 st from the bar between sts in pattern (either purlwise tbl or knitwise tbl).

After 26½ in (67 cm) (161 rows) from cast-on row, BO sts for shoulder sloping as follows: at both ends of the row, BO 3/5/5 sts once, and in every other row, BO 4 sts 4 times/BO 5 sts twice and BO 4 sts twice/BO 5 sts 4 times (55/55/57 sts).

After 1½ in (4 cm) (10 rows) from the beginning of the shoulder

RS row, and in every other row thereafter, before the bias band, p2tog, and after the bias band, inc 1 st from the bar between sts in pattern. When this bias band has traveled all the way to the right edge, continue working neckline decreases over the first 2 sts, at the same time continuing increases.

After 26½ in (67 cm) (161 rows) from cast-on row, for shoulder sloping, bind off sts at the left edge: BO 3/5/5 sts once; and then in every other row BO 4 sts, 5 times/5 sts, twice; and BO 4 sts, 3 times/5 sts, 5 times.

SLEEVES

Using US 9 (5.5 mm) needles, CO 39 sts. For the cuffs, work ribbing for 1 in (2.5 cm) (6 rows), beginning in the first row (WS) with selv st, p1, k1 and ending the row with k1, p1, selv st. Continue in half brioche stitch. For sleeve shaping, at both ends of the row, CO 1 st each as follows: in the following 6th

row, once; in every 6th row a total of 10 times; and 7 times in every 4th row a total of 7 times (75 sts). After 16¼ in (41.5 cm) (99 rows) from cuff, BO all 75 sts.

Work the second sleeve the same way.

FINISHING

Wet block pieces to indicated measurements and let dry.

Sew on the pocket linings from the inside.

For the front bands, using US 9 (5.5 mm) circular needle, pick up and knit sts as follows: 80 sts from each straight edge and 65 sts from each sloped neckline section (145 sts) and work ribbing, adding 3 buttonholes to the buttonhole band on the right front evenly distributed between the hem and the beginning of the sloped neckline section at ½ in (1 cm) front band height: In RS rows knit/purl together the 7th and 8th st in pattern, *34 sts ribbing pattern, k2tog/

p2tog 2 sts in pattern, repeat from * 2 times more. At the buttonholes, divide work and continue working over the individual sections separately. After 1 in (2.5 cm) buttonhole band height, work over all 145 sts again, casting on 1 new st each over each buttonhole. After 1¾ in (4.5 cm) buttonhole band height, BO all sts. Work the button band on the left front the same way, but without buttonholes.

Sew Fronts and Back together along the sloped shoulders, sewing the narrow sides of the front bands to the back neckline, too. Seam the sleeves to the sides of both shoulders over 8½ in (21.5 cm). Close the sleeve seams and side seams. Finally, sew on the 3 buttons.

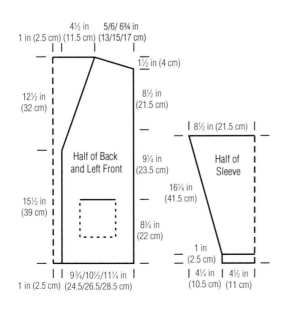

STOCKINETTE STITCH
In rows: knit on RS, purl on WS.
In rounds: knit all sts in all rounds.

STRIPE SEQUENCE
3 rnds in B (Lilac/Black) held with C (Orchid Mottled), *4 rnds in A (Cyclamen/Black) held with C (Orchid Mottled), 4 rnds in B (Lilac/Black) held with C (Orchid Mottled), repeat from *.

ACCENTED DECREASES
At the beginning of the row, after the first two sts, k2tog. At the end of the row, work to last 4 sts, then

At the markers, inc 1 st each (4 sts per round) at begin and end of Back and Front, for the first time in round 17 from cast-on row, then once in the following 14th round (round 31 from CO) as follows: *work to 3 sts after the imagined side seam, inc 1 st, work to 3 sts before next side seam, inc 1 st, repeat from * (98/104/110 sts).

At 12¼ in (31 cm) (45 rows) from cast-on row, divide for armholes at the imagined side seams (49/52/55 sts each for Front and Back) and continue first working the Front in back-and-forth rows.

last raglan decrease, BO the last 2 sts. Finish the Right Front the same way.

Now, continue working the Back. For raglan shaping, first BO 1 st each at both ends of the row at the beginning of the following RS and WS rows respectively, then work accented decreases of 1 st each in every other row 14 times total/in the following 4th row, once, and in every other row 14 times total/in the following 4th row, once, and in every other row 16 times total (19/20/19 sts). After the last raglan decrease, BO remaining sts.

PURPLERAIN SHIMMERING STRIPED SWEATER

sl1, k1, psso the 3rd- and 4th-to-last st, work 2 last sts.

INSTRUCTIONS

FRONT AND BACK
Front and Back are worked in the round up to the armholes.

With US 15 (10 mm) circular needle and 2 strands of yarn held together, 1 strand each of B and C, CO 90/96/102 sts. Join into round and work in stockinette stitch in stripe sequence. Mark the imagined side seams (beginning of round and half of round, 45/48/51 sts each for Front and Back).

For raglan shaping, first BO 1 st each at both ends of the row at the beginning of the following RS and WS rows respectively, then work accented decreases of 1 st each in every other row, 14 times total/in the following 4th row, once, and in every other row, 14 times total/in the following 4th row, once, and in every other row, 16 times total.

When armhole has reached a depth of 8/9¼/10½in (20.5/23.5/26.5 cm) (30/34/38 rows), BO the middle 16/15/16 sts for the neckline and finish the Left Front first.

At inside edge, in the following 2nd row, BO 1 st once. After the

SLEEVES
With US 15 (10 mm) circular needle and 2 strands of yarn held together, 1 strand each of B and C, CO 49/51/55 sts. Work in stockinette stitch in stripe sequence, beginning with 4 rows with 2 strands of yarn held together in B and C.

For the trumpet shape, dec 2 sts each in row 3 from cast-on row and later 6 times more in every 4th row as follows: sl1, k1, psso the 2 sts before the middle 17 sts, and k2tog the 2 sts after the middle 17 sts (35/37/41 sts).

At 8 in (20.5 cm) (30 rows) from cast-on row, for raglan shaping, first BO 1 st each at both ends of the row at the beginning of the following RS and WS rows respectively. Then work accented decreases of 1 st each in every 4th row, once/twice/twice, then in every other row, 12 times/12 times/14 times total.

After 8/9¼/10½ in (20.5/23.5/26.5 cm) (30/34/38 rows) from the beginning of the raglan shaping, BO remaining 7 sts.

Work the second sleeve the same way.

FINISHING

Wet block pieces to indicated measurements and let dry.

Sew the sleeves to the Front and Back along the raglan lines.

For the collar, using short US 13 (9 mm) circular needle and holding 2 strands of yarn together (1 strand each of B and C/A and C/B and C), pick up and knit 39 sts from the neckline edge, then work 36 rnds in stockinette stitch in stripe sequence, starting with 3 rnds B and C/A and C/B and C. Bind off all sts. Fold collar over in half toward the inside and sew on, making sure that neck opening won't turn out too small.

For sleeve cuffs, using short US 13 (9 mm) circular needle and holding 2 strands of yarn together (1 strand each of A and C), pick up and knit 49/51/55 sts from the bottom edge of each sleeve, work in stockinette stitch in stripe sequence for 32 rows, then BO all sts. Close sleeve and side seams. Fold sleeve cuffs over in half toward the inside and sew on.

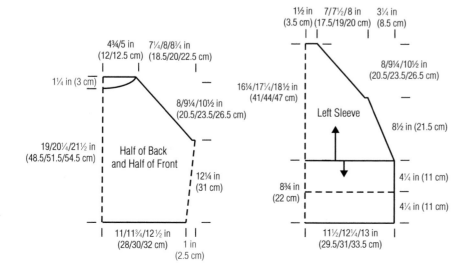

RIBBING
*K2, p2; repeat from *.

STOCKINETTE STITCH
Knit on RS, purl on WS.

DIAMOND PATTERN
Work from chart. Only RS rows are shown; in WS rows, work all sts as they appear (knit the knits and purl the purls). Work the pattern repeat (6 sts wide), repeating rows 1–12.

Pattern repeat = 6 sts

- = purl 1
- ■ = knit 1
- = hold 1 st on cable needle behind work, knit 1, then purl 1 from cable needle
- = hold 1 st on cable needle in front of work, purl 1, then knit 1 from cable needle

INSTRUCTIONS

BACK
Using US 4 (3.5 mm) needles, CO 142 sts. For bottom ribbing, work in ribbing pattern for 1½ in (4 cm), starting on a WS row with selv st, p1, and ending the row with p1, selv st. Change to US 6 (4 mm) needles and continue in stockinette stitch. At 15¾ in (40 cm) from bottom ribbing, mark the beginning of the armhole at both

REDROSES ROMANTIC DROP SHOULDER SWEATER

DIFFICULTY LEVEL 2

SIZES
Bust circumference in oversize fit: 36–42 in (91–107 cm)

Thanks to its relaxed shape, this garment will fit a range of sizes.

MATERIALS
- #4 medium-weight yarn; shown in Lana Grossa Alta Moda Superbaby Fine; 63% wool, 27% alpaca, 10% polyamide; 126 yd (115 m), 0.9 oz (25 g) per skein; #01 Bordeaux, 20 skeins
- US 4 (3.5 mm) and US 6 (4 mm) knitting needles
- US 4 (3.5 mm) circular knitting needle, 24 in (60 cm) long

GAUGE
In stockinette stitch on US 6 (4 mm) needles, 22 sts and 28 rows = 4 x 4 in (10 x 10 cm)

In diamond pattern on US 6 (4 mm) needles, 24 sts and 36 rows = 4 x 4 in (10 x 10 cm)

ends of the row and continue to work even. When armhole has reached a depth of 6¼ in (16 cm), BO 4 sts each for shoulder sloping at the beginning of the following RS and WS rows, then repeat binding off 4 sts 8 times more (4 sts bound off 9 times in all). In the following row, BO the remaining 70 sts for a straight edge.

FRONT
Using US 4 (3.5 mm) needles, CO 142 sts. For bottom ribbing, work in ribbing pattern for 1½ in (4 cm), starting on a WS row with selv st, p1, and ending the row with p1, selv st.

Change to US 6 (4 mm) needles and continue in stockinette stitch. After 14¼ in (36 cm) from bottom ribbing, mark the beginning of the armhole at both ends of the row and continue to work even. When armhole has reached a depth of

(continued) **REDROSES**

4 in (10 cm), BO the middle 36 sts for the neckline and continue both pieces separately. For further neckline shaping, bind off sts at the neck edge in every other row as follows: 5 sts once, 4 sts once, 3 sts once, 2 sts once, and 1 st 5 times in all. At neckline depth 2½ in (6 cm), place remaining 34 sts temporarily on a stitch holder and complete the other side the same way. Begin shoulder shaping by binding off 4 sts at both ends of the row once, and, AT THE SAME TIME, in the first row between the two sides, CO 70 new sts. Working over all sts together now, bind off more for shoulder sloping: at the beginning of every RS and WS row, BO 4 sts each 8 times more. After completion of shoulder shaping, BO the remaining 70 sts for a straight edge.

SLEEVES

Using US 6 (4 mm) needles, CO 56 sts. Work in diamond pattern, at first working the pattern repeat 9 times widthwise between selv sts. For sleeve shaping, inc 1 st each at both ends of the row, first time once in row 14 from cast-on row, then in every 14th row, twice, and in every 10th row, 8 times in all (78 sts). Incorporate the sts increased at both ends of the row into the established diamond pattern. After 18 in (46 cm) from cast-on row, BO all sts loosely.

Work the second sleeve the same way.

FINISHING

Wet block pieces to indicated measurements and let dry.

Sew Back and Front together at the sides up to the marked spots, making sure that Back below armhole is 1½ in (4 cm) shorter than Front. Sew the sloped shoulders and the straight edge in the middle completely to the Front; the seam will later end up on the back.

Using US 4 (3.5 mm) circular needle, pick up and knit 56 sts from the neckline edge. For neckline finishing, work in ribbing pattern in the round. At height of 1½ in (4 cm), BO sts in pattern, knit sts in knit and purl sts in purl.

Finally, close the sleeve seams and sew the sleeves into the armholes.

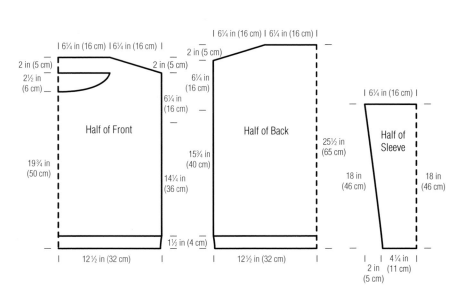

STOCKINETTE STITCH

Knit on RS, purl on WS.

MOSS STITCH

Row 1 (RS): Selv st, *k1, p1, repeat from * to last st, selv st.
Rows 2 and 4 (WS): Work the sts between selv sts as they appear: knit the knits and purl the purls.
Row 3: Selv st, *p1, k1, repeat from * to last st, selv st.
Repeat rows 1–4.

⟫⟫⟫ Work all parts with 5 strands of yarn held together, combining 2 strands of A (#4 medium-weight yarn) and 3 strands of B (#2 fine-weight yarn).

INSTRUCTIONS

BACK

Using US 11 (8 mm) needles and 5 strands of yarn held together as described, CO 84/89/94 sts. Work in moss stitch, starting on a WS row with selv st, p1. Shift the stitch pattern as described, starting in the following RS row and after this, shifting again in every other row.

At 7 in (18 cm) (33 rows) from cast-on row, for bell-shaped decreases, BO 1 st each at the beginning of the following RS and WS rows, then BO 1 st each at both ends of the row the same way in every 10th and 11th row, 7 times more; in every 6th and 7th row, 4 times more; and in every 4th and

SWEETLAVENDER SPARKLING MAKE-AN-ENTRANCE DUSTER

DIFFICULTY LEVEL 1

SIZES

Bust circumference for oversize fit: 36–38/40–42/44–46 in (91–97/102–107/112–117 cm)

Numbers for size 36–38 in (91–97 cm) are listed before the first slash, for 40–42 in (102–107 cm) between slashes, and for 44–46 in (112–117 cm) after the second slash. If only one number is given, it applies to all sizes.

MATERIALS

- Yarn A: #4 medium-weight yarn; shown in Lana Grossa Merino Air; 90% wool, 10% polyamide; 142 yd (130 m), 1.75 oz (50 g) per skein; #22 Eggplant, 17/18/19 skeins
- Yarn B: #2 fine-weight yarn; shown in Lana Grossa Lace Lux; 67% viscose, 33% wool; 339 yd (310 m), 1.75 oz (50 g) per skein; #36 Purple Mottled, 9/10/11 skeins
- US 11 (8 mm) knitting needles
- US 11 (8 mm) circular knitting needle, 48 in (120 cm) long
- US J/10 (6 mm) crochet hook

GAUGE

In moss stitch on US 11 (8 mm) needles with 2 strands of A (#4 medium-weight yarn) and 3 strands of B (#2 fine-weight yarn) held together, 11 sts and 18 rows = 4 x 4 in (10 x 10 cm)

In stockinette stitch on US 11 (8 mm) needles with 2 strands of A (#4 medium-weight yarn) and 3 strands of B (#2 fine-weight yarn) held together, 10.5 sts and 16 rows = 4 x 4 in (10 x 10 cm)

(continued) SWEETLAVENDER

5th row, 5 times more (50/55/60 sts).

AT THE SAME TIME, after 13½ in (34 cm) (63 rows) from cast-on row, mark the beginning of the armhole at both ends of the row and continue, working decreases as described before.

When armhole has reached a depth of 11 in (28 cm) (50 rows), mark the end of the armhole and continue. After 8 in (20 cm) (36 rows) from the second marked spot, BO sts for shoulder shaping at both ends of the row, always at the beginning of every RS and WS row: BO 2 sts, once; then in every other row, BO 2 sts each, 2 times more; then 4 sts, once; and 6/9/11 sts, once.

In the following row, BO the remaining 18/17/18 sts for the straight part of the neckline.

LEFT FRONT

With US 11 (8 mm) needles and 5 strands of yarn held together as described, CO 40/43/45 sts. Work in moss stitch, starting on a WS row with selv st, p1. Shift the stitch pattern as described, starting immediately in the next RS row and after this, shifting as described in every other row.

After 7 in (18 cm) (33 rows) from cast-on row, BO at the right edge for bell-shaped decreases: BO 1 st; then BO the same way in every 10th row 1 st each, 7 times more; in every 6th row, 4 times;

in every 4th row, 5 times more (23/26/28 sts).

AT THE SAME TIME, after 13½ in (34 cm) (63 rows) from cast-on row, at the right edge, mark the beginning of the armhole and continue, working decreases as described before. When armhole has reached a depth of 11 in (28 cm) (50 rows), mark the end of the armhole and continue.

At 24½ in (62 cm) (113 rows) from cast-on row, BO at the left edge for neckline shaping: BO 1 st once, then BO 1 st each in every 6th row 6 times more.

AT THE SAME TIME, at 8 in (20 cm) (36 rows) after the second marked spot, BO sts for shoulder shaping at the right edge: BO 2 sts, once; then in every other row, BO 2 sts each, 2 times more; then 4 sts, once; and 6/9/11 sts, once. All sts have now been used up.

RIGHT FRONT

With US 11 (8 mm) needles and 5 strands of yarn held together as described, CO 40/43/45 sts. Work in moss stitch, starting on a WS row with selv st, p1. Shift the stitch pattern as described, starting

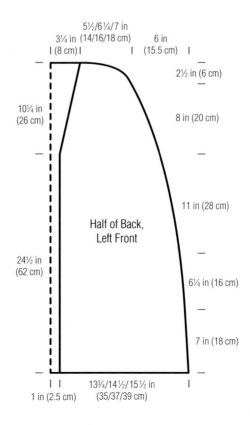

immediately in the next RS row and after this, shifting as described in every other row.

After 7 in (18 cm) (33 rows) from cast-on row, BO at the left edge for bell-shaped decreases: BO 1 st; then BO the same way 1 st each in every 10th row, 7 times more; in every 6th row, 4 times; and in every 4th row, 5 times more (23/26/28 sts).

AT THE SAME TIME, after 13½ in (34 cm) (63 rows) from cast-on row, at the left edge, mark the beginning of the armhole and continue, working decreases as described before. When armhole has reached a depth of 11 in (28 cm) (50 rows), mark the end of the armhole and continue.

At 24½ in (62 cm) (113 rows) from cast-on row, BO at the right edge for neckline shaping: BO 1 st once, then BO 1 st each in every 6th row 6 times more.

AT THE SAME TIME, at 8 in (20 cm) (36 rows) after the second marked spot, BO sts for shoulder shaping at the left edge: BO 2 sts, once; then in every other row, BO 2 sts, 2 times more; then 4 sts, once; and 6/9/11 sts, once. All sts have now been used up.

FINISHING

Wet block pieces to indicated measurements and let dry.

Sew together Fronts and Back at the shoulders up to the second marked spot. Leave armholes open between marked spots. Close remaining side seams, starting at the first marked spot to the cast-on row.

Now, with US 11 (8 mm) circular needle and 5 strands of yarn held together as described, pick up and knit sts: from the vertical edges of the Fronts, 65 sts each, from the sloped sections of the neckline, 29 sts each, and along the back neckline, 17 sts (205 sts). For the two-layered all-around edging, work 4 in (10 cm) as follows: 8 rows stockinette, then knit one WS row for the fold line, and work another 7 rows stockinette. Now, BO all sts loosely. Fold the all-around edging inward along the fold row and sew it on, including sewing the narrow sides of the edging at the hemline together to hide the selv sts inside. The finished edging is 2 in (5 cm) wide after folding.

With US J/10 (6 mm) crochet hook and 4 strands of yarn (1 strand A and 3 strands B) held together, further reinforce armhole edges by working 2 rnds of single crochet and 1 rnd of reverse single crochet (crab stitch) around, working the first single crochet round on the WS of the fabric and joining each rnd with a slip st.

GARTER STITCH
In rows: knit on RS, knit on WS.
In rounds: alternate 1 knit round and 1 purl round.

STOCKINETTE STITCH
Knit on RS, purl on WS.

SEED STITCH
Row 1: *K1, p1; repeat from *.
Row 2: *P1, k1; repeat from *.
Repeat rows 1–2, knitting the purls, and purling the knits in every row.

INSTRUCTIONS

BACK
Cast on 86/92 sts and, for the edging, work ¾ in (2 cm) (3 rows) garter stitch, starting with a WS row. Now, work even, dividing the sts of the row as follows: selv st, 33/36 sts stockinette, 18 sts seed stitch, 33/36 sts stockinette, selv st.

The seed stitch panel widens toward the shoulders because of taking over sts from the adjoining stockinette section, increasing sts before and after the panel, and decreasing again in the stockinette section. For this, work the following in every 12th row a total of 8 times: Work in stockinette to the last 2 sts of the stockinette section before the seed stitch panel; knit the last 2 stockinette sts together; make 1 from the bar between sts and knit it tbl; work the seed stitch panel; make 1 from the bar between sts and knit it tbl; work sl1, k1, psso on the first 2 sts of the stockinette sec-

GREENMOSS COUNTRY-STYLE TWEED SWEATER

DIFFICULTY LEVEL 1

SIZES
Bust circumference for oversize fit: 36–40/42–46 in (91–102/107–117 cm)

Numbers for size 36–40 in (91–97 cm) are listed before the slash, for size 42–46 in (107–117 cm) after the slash. If only one number is given, it applies to both sizes.

MATERIALS
- #5 bulky-weight yarn; shown in Lana Grossa Royal Tweed; 100% merino wool; 109 yd (100 m), 1.75 oz (50 g) per skein; #03 Loden Mottled, 9/10 skeins
- US 10.5/11 (7 mm) knitting needles
- US 10.5/11 (7 mm) circular knitting needle, 24 in (60 cm) long

GAUGE
In stockinette stitch on US 10.5/11 (7 mm) needles, 14 sts and 24 rows = 4 x 4 in (10 x 10 cm)

In seed stitch on US 10.5/11 (7 mm) needles, 15 sts and 23 rows = 4 x 4 in (10 x 10 cm)

tion after the seed st panel. Incorporate the additional sts into the seed stitch panel in subsequent rows. After completion, the seed stitch panel will be 34 sts wide, each stockinette section will have 25/28 sts (8 sts fewer per each than at the beginning).

AT THE SAME TIME, after 15 in (38 cm) (78 rows) from end of bottom edging, mark the beginning of the armhole at both ends of the row, and continue to work even. When armhole has reached a depth of 7/7½ in (18/19 cm) (36/38 rows), BO the middle 18 sts for the neckline and continue both parts separately. For further neckline shaping, at the neck-side edge, in the 2nd row, BO 3 sts once. At neckline depth of ¾ in (2 cm) (4 rows), BO remaining 31/34 shoulder sts. Finish the other side of the Back the same way, but mirror inverted.

(continued) GREENMOSS

FRONT

Work the same as the Back, but with a deeper neckline. For this, BO the middle 12 sts for the neckline and continue both parts separately when armhole depth has reached 4¾/5¼ in (12/13 cm) (24/26 rows). For further neckline shaping, at the inside (neck) edge, in every other row, BO 3 sts once, 2 sts once, and 1 st once. BO the remaining 31/34 shoulder sts at the outside edge at the same height as for the Back. Finish the other side of the Front the same way, but mirror inverted.

SLEEVES

Cast on 30/32 sts. For the sleeve edging, work garter stitch for ¾ in (2 cm) (3 rows), starting with a WS row. Now, continue in stockinette. For sleeve shaping, inc 1 st each at both ends of the row, for the first time in the 9th row from end of sleeve edging, then in every 6th row 9 times more (50/52 sts). After 14½ in (37 cm) (76 rows) from end of sleeve edging, BO all sts loosely.

Work the second sleeve the same way.

FINISHING

Wet block pieces to indicated measurements and let dry.

Sew Front and Back together at the shoulders and the sides, leaving the marked armholes open.

Using circular needle, pick up and knit 72 sts from the neckline edge and work neckline edging in garter stitch in the round for ¾ in (2 cm) (3 rnds), then BO all sts.

Lastly, seam the sleeves and sew the sleeves into the armholes.

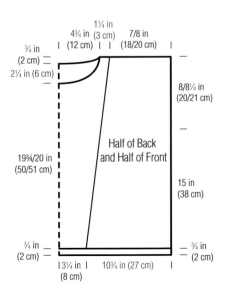

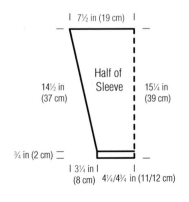

RIBBING
*K2, p2; repeat from *.

SLIPPED STITCH PATTERN
Work in back-and-forth rows with turning, following the chart. Stitches are shown as they are worked. Repeat the pattern repeat (4 sts wide) and end with the st after the pattern repeat. Repeat rows 1–8.

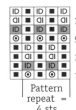

Pattern repeat = 4 sts

■ = knit 1

◉ = make a double yarn over and knit 1

ID = slip 1 purlwise with yarn in front of work, dropping the yarn overs from the previous row and pulling out an elongated stitch

ɑl = slip 1 purlwise with yarn in back of work

ID = slip 1 purlwise with yarn in front of work

COLOR SEQUENCE (FRONT AND BACK)
20 rows with C and F held together, 56 rows with E and F held together, 28 rows with D and F held together, 28 rows in B and F.

COLOR SEQUENCE (SLEEVES)
36 rows with C and F held together, 36 rows with D and F held together.

TEALBLUE BOYFRIEND SWEATER WITH COLOR BLOCKS

DIFFICULTY LEVEL 3

SIZES
Bust circumference in oversize fit: 38–42 in (96–107 cm)

Thanks to its generous shape, this garment will fit a range of sizes.

MATERIALS
■ #5 bulky-weight yarn; shown in Lana Grossa Royal Tweed; 100% merino wool; 109 yd (100 m), 1.75 oz (50 g) per skein; 1 skein #03 Loden Mottled (A), 2 skeins each #06 Anthracite Mottled (B) and #14 Gray Mottled (C), 3 skeins #77 Petrol Blue Mottled (D), and 4 skeins #76 Dark Petrol Mottled (E)

■ #4 medium-weight yarn; shown in Lana Grossa Garzato Fleece; 70% alpaca, 30% polyamide; 246 yd (225 m), 1.75 oz (50 g) per skein; #02 Petrol/Black, 6 skeins (F)

■ US 11 (8 mm) and US 13 (9 mm) knitting needles

■ US 10.5/11 (7 mm) and US 11 (8 mm) circular knitting needles

GAUGE
In slipped stitch pattern on US 13 (9 mm) needles with two strands of yarn held together, 13 sts and 19 rows = 4 x 4 in (10 x 10 cm)

(continued) TEALBLUE

INSTRUCTIONS

⟩⟩⟩ All parts are worked with two strands of yarn held together, combining 1 strand of #5 bulky-weight yarn with 1 strand of #4 medium-weight yarn.

BACK

With US 11 (8 mm) needles and A held together with F, CO 78 sts and work in ribbing pattern for 2 in (5 cm), starting the row with selv st, p1 and ending the row with p1, selv st. In the last WS row, inc 5 sts evenly distributed as follows: work 3 sts in pattern, *inc 1 st, work 15 sts in pattern, rep from * 4 times more (83 sts).

Change to US 13 (9 mm) needles and continue in slipped stitch pattern between the selv sts, staying in color sequence. At 19¼ in (49 cm) from bottom ribbing, mark the beginning of the armhole at both ends of the row. At overall height of approx. 29½ in (75 cm), BO all sts straight (after having completed the color sequence).

FRONT

Work the same as the Back, but for the neckline, at overall height of 27¼ in (69 cm), BO 9 center sts and finish both parts separately. For further neckline shaping, in every other row, bind off sts at the inside (neck) edge: 3 sts each, once; 2 sts each, twice; and 1 st each, once. At overall height of approx. 29½ in (75 cm), BO the remaining 29 shoulder sts.

SLEEVES

With US 11 (8 mm) needles and A held together with F, CO 26 sts and work in ribbing pattern for 2¾ in (7 cm), starting the row with selv st, p1 and ending the row with p1, selv st. In the last WS row, inc 9 sts evenly distributed as follows: work 4 sts in pattern, *inc 1 st, work 2 sts in pattern, rep from * 8 times more, work 4 sts in pattern (35 sts).

Change to US 13 (9 mm) needles and continue in slipped stitch pattern between the selv sts, staying in color sequence, making sleeve shaping increases of 1 st each at both ends of the row as follows: in every 8th row, twice, and in every 6th row, 9 times, incorporating these new sts into the stitch pattern (57 sts). At overall height of approx. 17¾ in (45 cm), BO all sts.

Work the second sleeve the same way.

FINISHING

Seam Front and Back at the shoulders.

For neckline edging, using US 11 (8 mm) circular needle and holding B together with F, pick up and knit 56 sts from the neckline edge and work in ribbing pattern. At a height of approx. 1¼ in (3 cm), change to US 10.5/11 (7 mm) needles and continue to approx. 2 in (5 cm) neckband height, then BO all sts loosely.

Sew the sleeves between the armhole markings, then close sleeve and side seams.

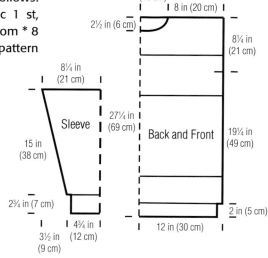

RIBBING
*K2, p2; repeat from *.

STOCKINETTE STITCH
Knit on RS, purl on WS.

CABLE PATTERN A
Work in rows from Chart A. Only RS rows are shown; in WS rows, work all sts as they appear (knit the knits and purl the purls). For width-wise row division, please refer to instructions on page 103. Row a is the next-to-last row of the ribbed cuff. In the first row of the chart, work increases as shown. Work rows 1–26 once, then repeat rows 3–26.

SUNDOWNER CABLED CARDIGAN WITH BAT SLEEVES

DIFFICULTY LEVEL 3

SIZES
Bust circumference in oversize fit: 36–44 in (91–112 cm)

Thanks to its relaxed shape, this garment will fit a range of sizes.

MATERIALS
- #6 super-bulky-weight yarn; shown in Lana Grossa Alta Moda Superbaby; 67% merino wool, 30% alpaca, 3% polyamide; 66 yd (60 m), 1.75 oz (50 g) per skein; #19 Red, 24 skeins

- US 10.5/11 (7 mm) and US 13 (9 mm) knitting needles
- US 10.5/11 (7 mm) circular knitting needle, 32 in (80 cm) long
- US 13 (9 mm) circular knitting needles, 32 in (80 cm) and 48 in (120 cm) long

GAUGE
50 sts in cable pattern A or B over the whole width on US 13 (9 mm) needles = approx. 13¾ in (35 cm)

In stockinette stitch on US 13 (9 mm) needles, 11 sts and 18 rows = 4 x 4 in (10 x 10 cm)

CHARTS PAGE 103

(continued) SUNDOWNER

CABLE PATTERN B

Work in rows from Chart B. Only RS rows are shown; in WS rows, work all sts as they appear (knit the knits and purl the purls). For width-wise row division, please refer to instructions. Row a is the next-to-last row of the ribbed cuff. In the first row of the chart, work increases as shown. Work rows 1–26 once, then repeat rows 3–26.

INSTRUCTIONS

LEFT FRONT WITH HALF A SLEEVE

Using US 10.5/11 (7 mm) needles, CO 34 sts. For bottom ribbing, work in ribbing pattern for 4 in (10 cm) (21 rows), starting with a WS row beginning with selv st, k2, and working the last 3 sts of the row as p2, selv st.

Change to US 13 (9 mm) needles and continue in cable pattern A as follows: selv st, work 32 sts of pattern repeat between arrows a and b, increasing 10 sts according to chart (42 sts), selv st.

At the right edge, inc 1 st each for bat sleeve shape, starting in row 3 from bottom ribbing, repeating increases in every 4th row, 15 times more; then in every other row, 10 times more (70 sts). Incorporate the first 8 increased sts into the cable pattern as shown between arrows a and c in the chart, working remaining 18 sts in stockinette stitch. Change to short US 13 (9 mm) circular needle as stitch count increases.

After 18½ in (47 cm) (84 rows) from bottom ribbing, continue sleeves, working even. At 6 in (15 cm) (28 rows) after last increase spot, place all sts on a stitch holder.

RIGHT FRONT WITH HALF A SLEEVE

Using US 10.5/11 (7 mm) needles, CO 34 sts. For bottom ribbing, work in ribbing pattern for 4 in (10 cm) (21 rows), starting on a WS row. Begin row with selv st, p2, and work last 3 sts of row as k2, selv st.

Change to US 13 (9 mm) needles and continue in cable pattern B as follows: selv st, 32 sts pattern repeat between arrows a and b, increasing 10 sts according to chart (42 sts), selv st.

At the left edge, inc 1 st each for bat sleeve shape, starting in row 3 from bottom ribbing, repeating increases in every 4th row, 15 times more; then in every other row, 10 times more (70 sts). Incorporate the first 8 increased sts into the cable pattern as shown between arrows b and c in the chart, working remaining 18 sts in stockinette stitch. Change to short US 13 (9 mm) circular needle as stitch count increases.

After 18½ in (47 cm) (84 rows) from bottom ribbing, continue sleeves, working even. At 6 in (15 cm) (28 rows) from last increase spot, place sts on a stitch holder.

〉〉〉 Arrows in the schematic indicate the knitting direction.

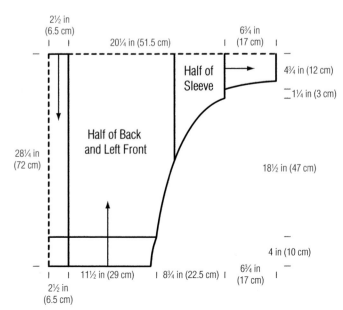

BACK

Transfer the formerly held sts of both Fronts to the longer US 13 (9 mm) circular needle, casting on 12 new sts between both Fronts (152 sts). Work these newly cast-on sts and both selv sts of both Fronts in stockinette stitch. To the right and left of this center panel, work both halves of the Back mirror inverted to the Fronts, continuing cable patterns A and B with the appropriate row.

After 6 in (15 cm) (28 rows) from the beginning of the Back, start decreases for bat sleeve shape. For this, BO 1 st each in every other row 11 times, then in every 4th row another 15 times (100 sts). In the last pattern row before the ribbed cuff, dec 10 sts each at both ends of the row over the cable pattern, reflecting the former increases in the Fronts (80 sts).

Change to US 10.5/11 (7 mm) needles to work bottom ribbing in back-and-forth rows, starting in row 1 with selv st, p2, and working the last 3 sts of the row as p2, selv st. When ribbing has reached a height of 4 in (10 cm) (20 rows), BO all sts in pattern, knit sts in knit and purl sts in purl.

FINISHING

Wet block the piece to indicated measurements and let dry.

Using longer US 10.5/11 (7 mm) circular and working from the center of the back neckline to the cast-on row of the Left Front, pick up and knit 91 sts. Work ribbed edge in back-and-forth rows, starting on a WS row with selv st, p2, and ending the row with p1, selv st. At a height of 2½ in (6.5 cm) (13 rows), BO sts in pattern, knit sts in knit and purl sts in purl. Work the other half of the ribbed edge the same way, but mirror inverted. Join both halves of the ribbed band in the center of the back neckline using mattress stitch.

Now, using US 10.5/11 (7 mm) circular needle, pick up and knit 32 sts each from the bottom edges of the sleeves. As setup for the sleeve cuff, purl one WS row, decreasing 6 sts evenly distributed as follows: p1, *p2tog, p3, rep from * 5 times more, p1 (26 sts). Now, work ribbing in back-and-forth rows, starting the next row with selv st, k1, and ending it with k1, selv st. When ribbing has reached a height of 6¾ in (17 cm), BO sts in pattern, knit sts in knit and purl sts in purl. Lastly, seam the underside edges of the sleeves and close the side seams.

BEIGE IS BEAUTIFUL

RIBBING
*K1, p1; repeat from *.

STAGGERED CUBE PATTERN
Work in back-and-forth rows with turning, following the chart. Stitches are shown as they appear from the RS of the fabric. Repeat rows 1–18. The pattern repeat is 8 sts wide.

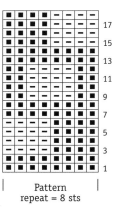

Pattern
repeat = 8 sts

▪ = knit 1 on RS; purl 1 on WS
▬ = purl 1 on RS; knit 1 on WS

GARTER STITCH SELVEDGE
Knit the first and last st of every row.

INSTRUCTIONS

Cast on 106 sts. Purl one WS row, then work 14 rows in ribbing pattern with garter stitch selvedge. Continue in staggered cube pattern for 110 rows. Finish off with 14 rows in ribbing pattern, then BO in pattern, working knit or purl sts.

FINISHING
Fold the rectangle in half crosswise, right sides facing inward, ribbing parts on top of each other. Starting from the ribbing, join the edges in mattress stitch over 8 in (20 cm) from both ends of the row. Turn the garment right side out.

DESERTDREAMS CAMEL JACKET

DIFFICULTY LEVEL 1

SIZES
Bust circumference in oversize fit: 36–40 in (91–102 cm)
Thanks to its relaxed shape, this garment will fit a range of sizes.

MATERIALS
- #5 bulky-weight yarn; shown in Lana Grossa Mille II; 50% merino wool, 50% acrylic; 61 yd (55 m), 1.75 oz/50 g per skein; #53 Camel, 12 skeins
- US 15 (10 mm) circular knitting needle

GAUGE
In staggered cube pattern on US 15 (10 mm) needles, 11 sts and 17 rows = 4 x 4 in (10 x 10 cm)

RIBBING

*K2, p1; repeat from *.

EYELET WAVE PATTERN

Work in rows from chart. Only RS rows are shown; in WS rows, purl all sts and yarn overs. Begin with the sts shown before the framed pattern repeat, repeat the pattern repeat (6 sts wide), ending the row with the sts shown after the framed pattern repeat. Repeat rows 1–8.

Pattern repeat = 6 sts

■ = knit 1

○ = yarn over

◣ = slip 1 knitwise, knit next st, pass slipped st over

− = purl 1

◢ = knit 2 sts together

PINK FLOWERS   SNUGGLY SWEATER IN PETAL COLORS

》》》 The sweater is worked with 3 strands of yarn held together throughout, combining 1 strand of medium-weight wool yarn with 1 strand each of light-weight mohair-silk yarn in both colors.

INSTRUCTIONS

BACK

With US 10 (6 mm) needles and 3 strands of yarn held together as described, CO 87/93 sts and work in eyelet wave pattern with 1 selv st each at begin and end of row. Before row 8, change to US 10.5/11 (7 mm) needles.

When piece has reached a height of 26 in (66 cm), BO sts for shoulder sloping at both ends of the row, as follows: at the begin-

DIFFICULTY LEVEL 2

SIZES

Bust circumference for oversize fit:
38–40/42–44 in (96–102/107–112 cm)

*Numbers for size 38–40 in (96–102 cm)
are listed before the slash, for size 42–44
in (107–112 cm) after the slash. If only one
number is given, it applies to both sizes.*

MATERIALS

- #4 medium-weight yarn; shown in
  Lana Grossa Bingo; 100% merino wool;
  87.5 yd (80 m), 1.75 oz (50 g) per
  skein; #168 Heather, 17/18 skeins

- #3 light-weight yarn; shown in Lana
  Grossa Silkhair; 70% mohair, 30% silk;
  230 yd (210 m), 0.9 oz (25 g) per
  skein; 5 skeins each in #35 Taupe and
  #58 Natural

- US 10 (6 mm) and US 10.5/11 (7 mm)
  knitting needles

- US 10 (6 mm) and US 10.5/11 (7 mm)
  circular knitting needles

GAUGE

In eyelet wave pattern on US 10.5/11
(7 mm) needles with 3 strands of yarn
held together (1 strand of medium-
weight wool yarn with 2 strands of light-
weight mohair-silk yarn), 15 sts and 17
rows = 4 x 4 in (10 x 10 cm)

ning of the next RS and WS rows, BO 8 sts each; then at the beginning of every following RS and WS rows, BO 7/8 sts each 3 times in all. Lastly, BO remaining 29 sts.

FRONT

Work the same as the Back, but for neckline shaping, at 24½ in (62 cm) overall height, BO 9 center sts and finish both parts separately. For further neckline shaping, bind off sts at the inside (neck) edge: 4 sts, once; 2 sts, twice; and 1 st, twice.

When piece has reached a height of 26 in (66 cm), BO 8 sts for shoulder sloping at the outside edges at the beginning of the next row, then at the beginning of every other row, BO 7/8 sts each, 3 times in all.

Work the other side of the front the same way.

SLEEVES

With US 10 (6 mm) needles and 3 strands of yarn, CO 39 sts and work in eyelet wave pattern. Before row 8, change to US 10.5/11 (7 mm) needles. For sleeve shaping, inc 1 st each at both ends of the row in every 6th row, 12 times (63 sts), incorporating the new sts into the lace pattern. At 17¾ in (45 cm) overall height, BO all sts.

Work the second sleeve the same way.

FINISHING

Seam Front and Back at the shoulders.

For the turtleneck collar, with US 10 (6 mm) circular needle and 3 strands of yarn held together, pick up and knit 57 sts from the neckline edge, and work in ribbing pattern in the round for 2½ in (6 cm), then change to US 10.5/11 (7 mm) needles and continue to approx. height of 12 in (30 cm), then BO all sts very loosely.

Sew the sleeves to the Back and Front so that the top center of the sleeve meets the shoulder seam. Lastly, close sleeve and side seams.

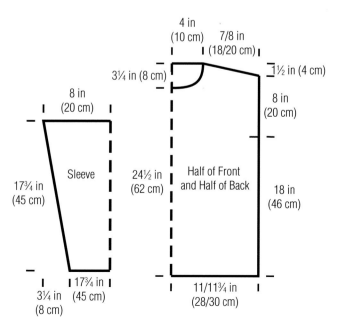

RIBBING

*K2, p2; repeat from *.

CHEVRON LACE

Work in rows from chart. Only RS rows are shown; in WS rows, purl all sts and yarn overs. Repeat the pattern repeat (10 sts wide), ending with the st after the pattern repeat. Repeat rows 1–4.

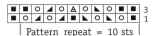

| Pattern repeat = 10 sts |

- ■ = knit 1
- ○ = yarn over
- ◣ = slip 1 knitwise, knit next st, pass slipped st over
- ◢ = knit 2 sts together
- ▲ = sl1, k2tog, pass slipped stitch over

INSTRUCTIONS

BACK

Using US 8 (5 mm) needles, CO 70/82 sts. For bottom ribbing, work in ribbing pattern for 3½ in (9 cm) (25 rows), starting on a WS row beginning with selv st, p1 and ending with p1, selv st. In the last row, inc 13/11 sts from the bar between sts evenly distributed, as follows: k5, *inc 1 st, k5/7, rep from * 12/10 times more (83/93 sts).

FINELACE DELICATE TOP WITH LACE

DIFFICULTY LEVEL 1

SIZES

Bust circumference for oversize fit: 36–38/44–46 in (91–97/112–117 cm)

Numbers for size 36–38 in (91–97 cm) are listed before the slash, for size 44–46 in (112–117 cm) after the slash. If only one number is given, it applies to both sizes.

MATERIALS

- #4 medium-weight yarn; shown in Lana Grossa Merino Air; 90% wool, 10% polyamide; 142 yd (130 m), 1.75 oz (50 g) per skein; #09 Light Beige, 6/7 skeins
- US 8 (5 mm) and US 10.5/11 (7 mm) knitting needles
- US 8 (5 mm) circular knitting needles, 16 in (40 cm) and 24 in (60 cm) long

GAUGE

In chevron lace pattern on US 10.5/11 (7 mm) needles, 14 sts and 20 rows = 4 x 4 in (10 x 10 cm)

Change to US 10.5/11 (7 mm) needles and continue in chevron lace pattern with selv sts at the beginning and end of the row. After 15¾ in (40 cm) (80 rows) from bottom ribbing, mark the beginning of the armhole at both ends of the row, then continue to work even. When armhole has reached a depth of 9½/9¾ in (24/25 cm) (48/50 rows), BO sts at both ends of the row for shoulder sloping, as follows: at the beginning of the next RS and WS rows, BO 4/3 sts each once; then BO 3/4 sts each 6 times more at the beginning of every RS and WS row. AT THE SAME TIME, at the next-to-last shoulder decrease, BO the middle 31 sts and continue both parts separately. For further neckline shaping, at the inside (neck) edge, in the following 2nd row, BO 4 sts once. With this, the sts on one side have been used up.

Finish the other side the same way, but mirror inverted.

FRONT

Using US 8 (5 mm) needles, CO 70/82 sts. For bottom ribbing, work in ribbing pattern for 3½ in (9 cm) (25 rows), starting on a WS row with selv st, p1 and ending the row with p1, selv st. In the last row, inc 13/11 sts from the bar between sts evenly distributed: k5, *inc 1 st, k5/7, rep from * another 12/10 times (83/93 sts).

Change to US 10.5/11 (7 mm) needles and continue in chevron lace pattern with selv sts at the beginning and end of the row. At 15¾ in (40 cm) (80 rows) from bottom ribbing, mark the beginning of the armhole at both ends of the row, then continue to work even.

When armhole has reached a depth of 4¼/4¾ in (11/12 cm) (22/24 rows), BO the middle 15 sts and continue both parts separately. For further neckline shaping, bind off sts in every other row at the inside (neck) edge: BO 3 sts once; 2 sts twice; 1 st twice; then 1 st each in every 4th row another 3 times.

At the same time, when armhole has reached a depth of 9½/9¾ in (24/25 cm) (48/50 rows), bind off sts at the outside for shoulder sloping: BO 4/3 sts once; then in every other row, BO 3/4 sts each 6 times more.

FINISHING

FINISHING

Wet block pieces to indicated measurements and let dry.

Sew Front and Back together at the shoulders and at the sides—at the sides only up to the marked spots.

Using short circular needle, pick up and knit 96/100 sts around each armhole edge. For armhole finishing, work ribbing in the round. At a height of 1½ in (4 cm), BO all sts loosely in pattern, knit sts in knit and purl sts in purl.

With long circular, pick up and knit 152 sts around the neckline edge. Work the neckband the same way as the armhole finishing.

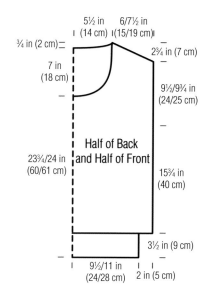

RIBBING

*K2, p2; repeat from *.

GARTER STITCH

In rows: knit on RS, knit on WS.

INSTRUCTIONS

BACK

Using US 13 (9 mm) needles, CO 56 sts and work in garter stitch. At 26½ in (67 cm) overall height, bind off for armhole shaping at both ends of the row, as follows: at the beginning of the next RS and WS rows, BO 5 sts each (46 sts). At 34 in (86 cm) overall height, BO sts for shoulder sloping at both ends of the row: at the beginning of the next RS and WS rows, BO 5 sts each the same way, BO another 5 sts each twice at both ends of the row. AT THE SAME TIME, at 34¼ in (87 cm) overall height of piece, BO the middle 6 sts for the neckline and finish both parts separately. For further neckline shaping, at the neck side edge, 5 sts once in the following 2nd row. All sts have now been used up. Work the other side the same way.

LEFT FRONT

Using US13 (9 mm) needles, CO 27 sts and work in garter stitch. At 26½ in (67 cm) overall height, BO 5 sts at the right edge for armhole shaping (22 sts).

At 26¾ in (68 cm) overall height, BO sts for neckline shaping at the left edge: BO 1 st once; then in every 4th row, BO 1 st twice; in every 6th row, BO 1 st 4 times. AT THE SAME TIME, at 34 in (86 cm) overall height, bind off sts at the right edge in every other row for shoulder sloping: BO 5 sts each, 3 times total.

THINK**BIG** STYLISH CHUNKY KNIT COAT

DIFFICULTY LEVEL 1

SIZES

Bust circumference in oversize fit: 36–40 in (91–102 cm)

Thanks to its relaxed shape, this garment will fit a range of sizes.

MATERIALS

- #6 super-bulky-weight yarn; shown in Lana Grossa Lei; 100% merino wool yarn; 44 yd (40 m), 1.75 oz (50 g) per skein; #14 Raw White, 30 skeins
- US 13 (9 mm) knitting needles
- US 11 (8 mm) and US 13 (9 mm) circular knitting needles

GAUGE

In garter st on US 13 (9 mm) needles, 9 sts and 16 rows = 4 x 4 in (10 x 10 cm)

RIGHT FRONT

Using US 13 (9 mm) needles, CO 27 sts and work in garter stitch. At 26½ in (67 cm) overall height, BO 5 sts at the left edge for armhole shaping (22 sts).

At 26¾ in (68 cm) overall height, BO sts for neckline shaping at the right edge: BO 1 st once; then in every 4th row, BO 1 st twice; in every 6th row, BO 1 st 4 times. AT THE SAME TIME, at 34 in (86 cm) overall height, bind off sts at the left edge in every other row for shoulder sloping: BO 5 sts each 3 times total.

SLEEVES

Using US 13 (9 mm) needles, CO 24 sts and work in garter stitch. For sleeve shaping, inc 1 st each at both ends of the row in every 12th row, 6 times total (36 sts). At 21 in (53 cm) overall height, BO all sts. Work the second sleeve the same way.

FINISHING

Along the straight edge of the Right Front, using US 13 (9 mm) circular needle, pick up and knit 72 sts and work in ribbing pattern between the selv sts, starting with a WS row at the top edge and beginning every row with selv st, p2, k2. Now, work in short rows: after having worked the selv st and 8 more sts, then turn, make a yarn over onto the needle, and work back in pattern on the other side over these 9 sts. In the following row, turn 8 sts later than in the previous row (again with a yarn over). While staying in the ribbing pattern and always either knitting or purling the yarn over together with the following st, repeat these steps 5 more times, and for the 6th time, turn 7 sts later than in the previous row.

Finally, work one RS row over all sts. Now, work in ribbing pattern over all sts for 2 in (5 cm), then BO all sts.

Work the left band as for the Right Front, mirror inverted, beginning the short rows with 7 sts and ending with 9 sts.

Sew Fronts to Back at shoulders.

For the collar, using US 11 (8 mm) needles, pick up and knit 72 sts along the back neckline and the sloped sections of the Fronts, and work in ribbing pattern between the selv sts. At a height of 2 in (5 cm), change to US 13 (9 mm) needles. At approx. height of 7 in (18 cm), BO all sts loosely.

Sew the narrow sides of the collar to the front bands over 4 in (10 cm). Close side and sleeve seams and sew sleeves into armholes.

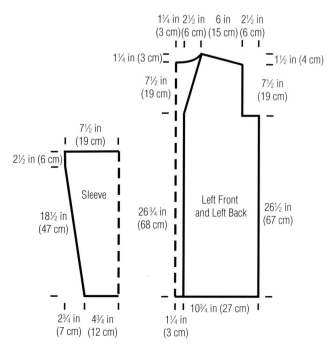

RIBBING
*K2, p2; repeat from *.

STOCKINETTE STITCH
In rnds: knit all sts.

DIAMOND LATTICE PATTERN
In rows: Work in rows from chart. Only RS rows are shown; in WS rows, purl all sts. Begin with the sts shown before the framed pattern repeat, repeat the pattern repeat (4 sts wide) and end with the sts shown after the framed pattern repeat. Repeat rows 1–8 all the time.

In rounds: Work odd-numbered rounds as in the chart; knit all sts in even-numbered rounds.

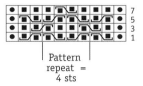

Pattern repeat = 4 sts

● = 1 selvedge stitch
▉▉ = hold 1 st on cable needle in front of work, knit 1, then knit 1 from cable needle
▉/▉ = hold 1 st on cable needle behind work, knit 1, then knit 1 from cable needle
■ = knit 1

INSTRUCTIONS

BACK WITH SHORT SLEEVES
With A, CO 46/54 sts. Knit 1 row on the WS, then continue in diamond lattice pattern.

After 4¾/5½ in (12/14 cm) (21/25 rows) from cast-on row, increase for sleeve extensions at both ends of the row, always at the beginning of a RS and WS row, as follows: 1 st each once; then in the 4th row, 1 st once; in every other row, 1 st each, 7 times; then 2 sts each, twice; and 3 sts each, once (78/86 sts), incorporating the

HONEYMILK FEMININE DIAMOND LATTICE SWEATER

DIFFICULTY LEVEL 2

SIZES
Bust circumference for oversize fit: 36–38/40–42 in (91–97/102–107 cm)

Numbers for size 36–38 in (91–97 cm) are listed before the slash, for size 40–42 in (102–107 cm) after the slash. If only one number is given, it applies to both sizes.

MATERIALS
■ Yarn A: #6 super-bulky-weight yarn; shown in Lana Grossa Alta Moda Superbaby; 67% merino wool, 30% alpaca, 3% polyamide; 66 yd (60 m), 1.75 oz (50 g) per skein; #09 Grège, 9/10 skeins

■ Yarn B: #3 light-weight mohair/silk yarn; shown in Lana Grossa Silkhair Melange; 70% mohair, 30% silk; 230 yd/210 m, 0.9 oz/25 g per skein; #701 Grège, 1 skein

■ US 15 (10 mm) circular knitting needle

■ US 15 (10 mm) set of double-pointed needles (DPN)

GAUGE
In diamond lattice pattern on US 15 (10 mm) needles and super-bulky yarn (A), 12.5 sts and 18 rows = 4 x 4 in (10 x 10 cm)

(continued) HONEYMILK

new sts into the diamond lattice pattern.

After the last sleeve extension increases, continue to work even. When sleeves have reached a height of 6¼ in (16 cm) (30 rows), place sts on a stitch holder at both ends of the row as follows and work short rows for shoulder shaping: At the beginning of the next RS and WS rows, hold 2/4 sts each, then hold 3 sts each, 6 times/4 sts each, twice and 3 sts each, 4 times, always turning with a yarn over and working back on the other side. Then, work a full row over all sts, always k2tog/ssk the former yarn over with the following st to avoid holes. Now, hold sts again at both ends of the row: 20/24 sts each for the shoulders and the middle 38 sts for the neckline.

FRONT WITH SHORT SLEEVES
Work the same as the Back.

FINISHING
Wet block pieces to indicated measurements and let dry.

Graft shoulder seams in Kitchener stitch over 20/24 sts for each shoulder.

Now, with US 15 (10 mm) DPN set, pick up and knit 2 times 38 sts from the neckline edge (76 sts total). Work the stand-up collar with A in the round, continuing the diamond lattice pattern and working intermittent rounds in knit. When collar has reached 2½ in (6 cm) (12 rnds), add another 4 rnds stockinette stitch in B, then BO all sts loosely.

Close sleeve and side seams.

Now, with US 15 (10 mm) DPN set and A, pick up and knit 46 sts around each armhole edge. For armhole finishing, work in ribbing pattern in the round, starting with k1 and ending with k1. When ribbing has reached 1½ in (4 cm), BO all sts in pattern, knit sts in knit and purl sts in purl.

>>> Arrows in the schematic indicate the knitting direction.

1 in (2.5 cm)
2½ in (6 cm)

6 in (15 cm)

6/7¼ in (15.5/18.5 cm)

1½ in (4 cm)

3½ in (8.5 cm)

3¼ in (8 cm)

Half of Sleeve

6¼ in (16 cm)

Half of Back and Half of Front

19¾/20½ in (50/52 cm)

5½ in (14 cm)

4¾/5½ in (12/14 cm)

7/8¼ in (18/21 cm)

5 in (12.5 cm)

1½ in (4 cm)

CHAINED EDGE

Knit the first st of every row through the back loop. Slip the last st of every row purlwise with yarn in front of work.

》》》Work chained edge at the open edges of the Fronts.

GARTER STITCH SELVEDGE

Slip the first st of every row knitwise. Knit the last st of every row.

BROKEN SEED STITCH

RS rows: purl.
WS rows: selv st, alternate k1, p1 to last st, selv st.

GARTER STITCH

In rows: knit on RS, knit on WS.

BROKEN SEED STITCH A

Work in back-and-forth rows from Chart A; row 1 is a WS row. Stitches are shown as they are worked. Each row starts and ends with a selv st. Between selv sts, work pattern repeat between arrows a and c/b and d. Work rows 1–3 once, then repeat only rows 2 and 3 a total of 5 times. End with rows 14 and 15. Work the selv sts as garter stitch selvedge.

SANDDUNES SNAZZY EVERYDAY COAT

DIFFICULTY LEVEL 3

SIZES

Bust circumference for oversize fit: 36–38/40–42 in (91–97/102–107 cm)

Numbers for size 36–38 in (91–97 cm) are listed before the slash, for size 40–42 in (102–107 cm) after the slash. If only one number is given, it applies to both sizes.

MATERIALS

- #6 super-bulky-weight yarn; shown in Lana Grossa Alta Moda Superbaby; 67% merino wool, 30% alpaca, 3% polyamide; 66 yd (60 m), 1.75 oz (50 g) per skein; #24 Beige, 20/21 skeins
- US 13 (9 mm) and US 15 (10 mm) knitting needles

GAUGE

In either cable pattern A or B on US 15 (10 mm) needles, 13 sts and 17.5 rows = 4 x 4 in (10 x 10 cm)

CHARTS PAGES 104–107

(continued) SANDDUNES

CABLE PATTERN B

Work in rows from Chart B. Only RS rows are shown; in WS rows, knit all sts between the selv sts. Widthwise, work pattern repeat between arrows a and c/b and d once. Work rows 1–34 once, then work only rows 11–34 twice, ending with rows 83–126/83–128.

For both sizes, work armhole shaping decreases from row 89 on at both ends of the row as shown immediately after the selv st (at beg of row) or before it (at end of row). In row 99, for size 36–38 in

(91–97 cm), work the purl st with gray background at both ends of the row as p2tog instead of sl1, k1, psso or k2tog; for size 40–42 in (102–107 cm) work as shown. Work the selv sts as garter stitch selvedge.

BROKEN SEED STITCH C

Work in back-and-forth rows from Chart C; row 1 is a WS row. Stitches are shown as they are worked. Between selv sts, work pattern repeat between arrows b and c/b and d once. Work rows 1–3 once,

then work only rows 2 and 3 a total of 5 times. End with rows 14 and 15. Work the selv sts as garter stitch selvedge.

CABLE PATTERN D

Work from Chart D in back-and-forth rows. Only RS rows are shown; in WS rows, knit all sts between the selv sts. Incorporate the 4 newly added sts with gray background, at the left edge, between arrows a and b, into the broken seed stitch pattern. Widthwise, work pattern repeat between arrows b and c/b and d once. Work rows 1–34 once, then work only rows 11–34 twice, ending with rows 83–126/83–128.

For both sizes, work armhole shaping decreases from row 89 on both ends of the row as shown immediately after (at beg of row) or before (at end of row) the selv st. In row 99, for size 36–38 in (91–97 cm), work the purl st with gray background at both ends of the row as p2tog instead of sl1, k1, psso; for size 40–42 in (102–107 cm) work as shown. Work the selv sts as garter stitch selvedge.

Rows 127–138/129–140 show half of the collar. Work these rows, too, only once. Work the selv sts at the right edge as garter stitch selvedge, at the left edge as chained edge.

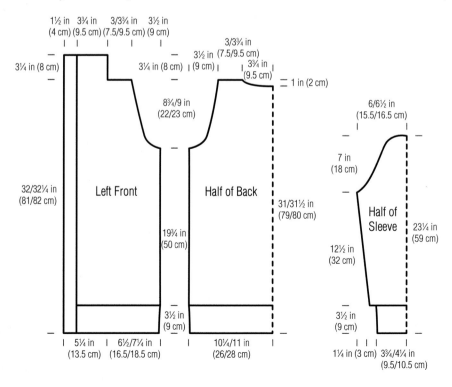

BROKEN SEED STITCH E

Work in back-and-forth rows from Chart E; row 1 is a WS row. Stitches are shown as they are worked.

Every row starts and ends with a selv st. Between selv sts, work pattern repeat between arrows a and c/b and d. Work rows 1–3 once, then work only rows 2 and 3 a total of 5 times. End with rows 14 and 15. Work the selv sts as garter stitch selvedge.

CABLE PATTERN F

Work in back-and-forth rows from Chart F. Only RS rows are shown; in WS rows, knit all sts between the selv sts. Width-wise, work pattern repeat between arrows a and c/b and d once. Work rows 1–88 once, including increases and decreases as shown. Work the selv sts as garter stitch selvedge.

BROKEN SEED STITCH G AND CABLE PATTERN H

Work the same as broken seed stitch E and cable pattern F from the appropriate charts.

INSTRUCTIONS

▶▶▶ All edges except those on the Fronts are worked with garter stitch selvedge.

BACK

Using US 13 (9 mm) needles, CO 63/67 sts. For bottom ribbing, work 3½ in (9 cm) (15 rows) in broken seed stitch A, starting with a WS row. In the last row, inc 8 times by making a yarn over as shown in the chart (71/75 sts).

Change to US 15 (10 mm) needles and continue in cable pattern B. After 19¾ in (50 cm) (88 rows) from bottom ribbing, make accented decreases of 1 st each at both ends of the row for armhole shaping as shown in the chart. Repeat these decreases in every other row 4 times more; and for the 5th time, during the last decrease, as described, work sl1, k1, psso or ssp decrease (59/63 sts).

Now, continue to work even. In row 107, at both ends of the row, reduce outmost cables by decreasing 7 sts each as shown in the chart (45/49 sts).

When armhole has reached a depth of 8/8¼ in (20/21 cm) (34/36 rows) or in row 123/125 of Chart B respectively, BO the middle 17 sts for the neckline and continue both parts separately. For further neckline shaping, at the inside (neck) edge, in the 2nd row, BO another 5 sts once. After row 126/128, BO remaining 9/11 shoulder sts. Finish the other side the same way.

LEFT FRONT

Using US 13 (9 mm) needles, CO 37/39 sts. For bottom ribbing, work 3½ in (9 cm) (15 rows) in broken seed stitch C, starting with a WS row as shown in the chart. In the last row, inc 4 times by making a yarn over each time (41/43 sts).

Change to US 15 (10 mm) needles and continue in cable pattern D. As shown in the chart, place the armhole at the right edge at the same height as on the Back (35/37 sts). Later, reduce the right cable by 7 sts at the same height as on the Back as shown in the chart (28/30sts).

When armhole has reached a depth of 8¾/9 in (22/23 cm) (38/40 rows), or after row 126/128, BO 8/10 sts at the right edge for the shoulder as shown in the chart, and over the remaining 20 sts, work 12 rows more for one half of the collar, to row 138/140 of Chart D, then BO all sts.

126/128, BO 8/10 sts at the left edge for the shoulder as shown in the chart, and over the remaining 20 sts, work 12 rows more for one half of the collar, to row 138/140 of Chart D, then BO all sts.

LEFT SLEEVE

Using US 13 (9 mm) needles, CO 27/29 sts. For the cuff, work 3½ in (9 cm) (15 rows) in broken seed stitch E, starting with a WS row as shown in the chart. In the last row, inc 8 times as shown by making a yarn over each time (35/37 sts).

Change to US 15 (10 mm) needles and continue in cable pattern F. For sleeve shaping, at both ends of the row, work accented increase of 4 sts each as shown, placing the inc 2 sts in from the edge for all sizes (43/45 sts). After 12½ in (32 cm) (56 rows) from bottom ribbing, at both ends of the row, make an accented decrease of 1 st each for the sleeve cap before/after the selv st as shown, then dec 1 st each the same way in every other row 3 times more. In the cable crossings, additionally dec 7 sts each 3 times more as shown. After row 88 of Chart F, BO remaining 14/16 sts.

RIGHT SLEEVE

Using US 13 (9 mm) needles, CO 27/29 sts. For the cuff, work 3½ in

RIGHT FRONT

Using US 13 (9 mm) needles, CO 37/39 sts. For bottom ribbing, work 3½ in (9 cm) (15 rows) in broken seed stitch C, starting with a WS row as shown in the chart. In the last row, inc 4 times by making a yarn over each time (41/43 sts).

Change to US 15 (10 mm) needles and continue in cable pattern D, but cross the cables mirror inverted to the right, as done for the left half of the Back. As shown in the chart, place the armhole at the right edge at the same height as on the Back (35/37 sts). Later, reduce the left cable by 7 sts at the same height as on the Back as shown in the chart (28/30 sts).

When armhole has reached a depth of 8¾/9 in (22/23 cm) (38/40 rows), or after row

(9 cm) (15 rows) in broken seed stitch G, starting with a WS row as shown in the chart. In the last row, inc 8 times as shown by making a yarn over each time (35/37 sts).

Change to US 15 (10 mm) needles and continue in cable pattern H. For sleeve shaping, at both ends of the row, work accented increase of 4 sts each as shown, placing the inc 2 sts in from the edge for all sizes (43/45 sts). After 12½ in (32 cm) (56 rows) from bottom ribbing, at both ends of the row, make an accented decrease of 1 st each side for the sleeve cap before/after the selv st as shown, then dec 1 st each side the same way in every other row 3 times more. In the cable crossings, additionally dec 7 sts each 3 times more as shown. After row 88 of Chart H, BO remaining 14/16 sts.

FINISHING

Wet block all pieces to indicated measurements and let dry.

Sew Fronts to Back along the shoulders and at the sides. Seam the collar in the center back. Sew the inner edge of the collar to the back neckline. Lastly, close the sleeve seams and sew the sleeves into the armholes.

RIBBING
*K1, p1; repeat from *.

HALF BRIOCHE STITCH
Work in rows from chart. Stitches are shown as they are worked. Begin with the sts shown before the framed pattern repeat, repeat the pattern repeat (2 sts wide) all the time, and end with the sts shown after the framed pattern repeat. Work rows 1–3 only once, then repeat rows 2–3. Row 1 is a WS row.

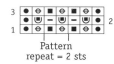

Pattern
repeat = 2 sts

• = 1 selvedge stitch

⊖ = slip 1 stitch purlwise with yarn in front + 1 yarn over

■ = knit 1

⊍ = knit 1 yarn over together with the following stitch

— = purl 1

STOCKINETTE STITCH
Knit on RS, purl on WS.

ACCENTED DECREASES
Decreasing 1 st: Work the first 4 sts of the row as selv st, 1 st stockinette, p2tog. Work the last 4 sts of the row as p2tog, 1 st stockinette, selv st.

Decreasing 2 sts: Work the first 5 sts of the row as selv st, 1 st stockinette, p3tog. Work the last 5 sts of the row as p3tog, 1 st stockinette, selv st.

SUGAR**BABE** CLASSIC CARDIGAN IN HALF BRIOCHE

DIFFICULTY LEVEL 3

SIZES
Bust circumference for oversize fit: 36–40/42–46 in (91–102/107–117 cm)

Numbers for size 36–40 in (91–102 cm) are listed before the slash, for size 42–46 in (107–117 cm) after the slash. If only one number is given, it applies to both sizes.

MATERIALS
- #6 super-bulky-weight yarn; shown in Lana Grossa Yak Merino; 30% merino wool, 28% alpaca, 22% polyamide, 20% yak; 120 yd (110 m), 1.75 oz (50 g) per skein; #10 Grège, 11/12 skeins
- #3 light-weight yarn; shown in Lana Grossa Lace Pearls; 30% wool, 26% polyamide, 18% mohair, 18% alpaca, 8% pearls; 150 yd (137 m), 0.9 oz (25 g); #103 Raw White/Grège/Sand, 9/10 skeins
- US 10.5/11 (7 mm) and US 11 (8 mm) knitting needles

GAUGE
In half brioche stitch on US 11 (8 mm) needles with two strands of yarn held together (1 strand each of both yarns), 12 sts and 20 rows = 4 x 4 in (10 x 10 cm)

(continued) SUGARBABE

ACCENTED INCREASES

Increase of 2 sts: Work the first 3 sts of the row as selv st, 1 st stockinette, 3 from 1 [k1-tbl, p1, and k1-tbl into the same st]. Work the last 3 sts of the row as: 3 from 1 [k1-tbl, p1, and k1-tbl into the same st], 1 st stockinette, selv st.

>>> The whole cardigan is worked with 2 strands of yarn held together, 1 strand each of both yarns.

INSTRUCTIONS

BACK

Using US 10.5/11 (7 mm) needles and 2 strands of yarn held together as described, CO 69/75 sts. For the bottom ribbing, work in ribbing pattern for 1¼ in (3 cm) (5 rows), starting with a RS row. Begin this row with selv st, k1 and end it with k1, selv st.

Change to US 11 (8 mm) needles and continue in half brioche stitch, beginning with a WS row as shown. For hip shaping, BO 1 st each at the beginning of rows 14 and 15 from end of bottom ribbing, then in every following 14th and 15th row, BO 1 st each 4 times more (59/65 sts).

After 15½ in (39 cm) (78 rows) from end of bottom ribbing, mark both ends of the row for the waist. In row 9 after the marked row,

inc 1 st each at both ends of the row for the upper body, then inc 1 st each again in every 8th row 2 times more (65/71 sts). Incorporate the new sts gained from the increases at both ends of the row into the half brioche stitch pattern. Before and after the selv st, you now have 1 knit st in the brioche pattern again.

After 7½/6¾ in (19/17 cm) (38/34 rows) after the marked row, start raglan shaping at both ends of the row as follows: in the following RS row, make an accented decrease of 2 sts; then in every 4th row, accent decrease 2 sts 5/8 times more; and in every 6th row, accent decrease 2 sts 4/2 times more. For size 42–46 in (107–117 cm) only, BO 1 st once in the following 4th row by p2tog the 3rd with the 4th st of the row and the 4th-to-last with the 3rd-to-last st of the row.

At raglan height of 8¾/9½ in (22/24 cm) (44/48 rows), BO middle 15 sts for the neckline and continue both parts separately. For further neckline shaping, at the inside (neck) edge, in the 2nd row, BO 2 sts once more. At raglan height of 9½/10¼ in (24/26 cm) (48/52 rows), BO the remaining 3 sts. Finish the other side the same way.

LEFT FRONT

With US 11 (8 mm) needles and yarn held double, CO 16/18 sts.

Work in half brioche stitch from the very beginning, starting on a WS row with selv st, k1. At the left edge, in the 2nd row from cast-on row, make an accented increase of 2 sts for hip shaping; then in every other row, accent increase 2 sts twice; in every 4th row, accent increase 2 sts each, 3 times in all; in the 6th row, accent increase 2 sts once; and in the 8th row accent increase 2 sts once more. You will have increased a total of 16 sts, and on the RS of the fabric, at the left edge, there is always a purl st before the selv st.

At the right edge, in the 10th row from end of bottom ribbing, BO 1 st for hip shaping; then in every following 14th row, BO 1 st each 4 times more (27/29 sts).

At the same height and in the same way as for the Back, mark the waist at the right edge of the piece. Then, at the right edge, inc 1 st each for the upper body the first time in row 9 after the marked row, then again in every 8th row 2 times more (30/32 sts). Incorporate the increased sts into the half brioche pattern.

After 22/21¼ in (56/54 cm) (112/108 rows) from cast-on row, make an accented decrease of 2 sts for raglan shaping at the right edge; then repeat accent decrease of 2 sts each in every 4th row 4/8 times more and in every 6th row 3/0 times more. For size 42–46 in

(107–117 cm) only, in the following 6th row, dec 1 st once as for the Back.

AT THE SAME TIME as the beginning of the raglan shaping, make neckline decreases at the left edge: accent decrease 2 sts once, then in every 6th row accent decrease 2 sts each 4 times more, placing the decreases always before the last knit st at the left edge.

At raglan height of 7½/8¼ in (19/21 cm) (38/42 rows), BO remaining 4/3 sts.

RIGHT FRONT

With US 11 (8 mm) needles and yarn held double, CO 16/18 sts. Work in half brioche stitch from the very beginning, starting on a WS row with selv st, k1. At the right edge, in the 2nd row from cast-on row, make an accented increase of 2 sts for hip shaping; then in every other row, accent increase 2 sts twice; in every 4th row, accent increase 2 sts each, 3 times in all; in the 6th row, accent increase 2 sts once; and in the 8th row accent increase 2 sts once more. You will have increased a total of 16 sts, and on the RS of the fabric, at the right edge, there is always a purl st after the selv st.

At the left edge, in the 10th row from end of bottom ribbing, BO 1 st for hip shaping, then in every following 14th row, BO 1 st each 4 times more (27/29 sts).

(continued) SUGARBABE

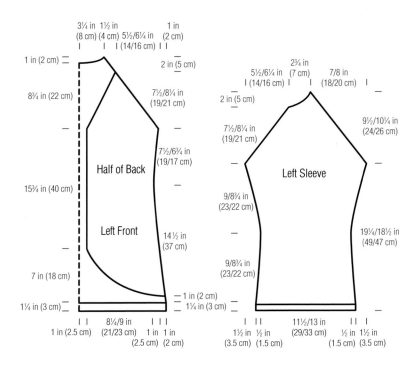

At the same height and in the same way as for the Back, mark the waist at the left edge of the piece. Then, at the left edge, inc 1 st each for the upper body the first time in row 9 after the marked row, then again in every 8th row 2 times more (30/32 sts). Incorporate the increased sts into the half brioche pattern.

After 22/21¼ in (56/54 cm) (112/108 rows) from cast-on row, make an accented decrease of 2 sts for raglan shaping at the left edge, then repeat accent decrease of 2 sts each in every 4th row 4/8 times more and in every 6th row 3/0 times more. For size 42–46 in (102–107 cm) only, in the follow-ing 6th row, dec 1 st once as for the Back.

AT THE SAME TIME as the beginning of the raglan shaping, make neckline decreases at the right edge: accent decrease 2 sts once, then in every 6th row accent decrease 2 sts each 4 times more, placing the decreases always after the first knit st at the right edge. At raglan height of 7½/8¼ in (19/21 cm) (38/42 rows), BO remaining 4/3 sts.

LEFT SLEEVE

With US 10.5/11 (7 mm) needles and yarn held double, CO 41/45 sts. For the bottom ribbing, work in ribbing pattern for 1¼ in (3 cm)

(5 rows), starting with a RS row beginning with selv st, k1 and end-ing with k1, selv st.

Change to US 11 (8 mm) nee-dles and continue in half brioche stitch, beginning with a WS row as shown. At both ends of the row, BO 1 st each for the trumpet shape in the 21st and 41st row from end of cuff (37/41 sts).

After 9/8¾ in (23/22 cm) (46/44 rows) from end of cuff, mark both ends of the row. For sleeve shaping, inc 1 st each at both ends of the row for the first time in the 7th row after the marked row, then in every 6th row 5 times more (49/53 sts). Incorpo-rate the new sts gained from the increases at both ends of the row into the half brioche stitch pattern.

After 9/8¾ in (23/22 cm) (46/44 rows) after the marked row, start raglan shaping at the right edge of the piece as follows: in the following RS row, make an accented decrease of 2 sts; then in every 4th row, accent decrease 2 sts, 5/8 times more; and in every 6th row, accent decrease 2 sts, 4/2 times more. For size 42–46 in (107–117 cm) only, in the fol-lowing 4th row, BO 1 st more once by p2tog the 3rd and 4th st of the row. AT THE SAME TIME, at the left edge, for raglan shaping, make an accented decrease of 2 sts, then repeat accent decrease of 2 sts each in every 4th row, 4/8 times more, and in every 6th row, 3/0 times more. For size 42–46 in

(107–117 cm) only, in the following 6th row, dec 1 st once as for the Back.

At 7½/8¼ in (19/21 cm) (38/42 rows) raglan height, BO 3 sts at the left edge for the neckline; then in every other row, BO 2 sts, 3 times more; and BO 1 st, once. After the last raglan decrease, at the right edge, BO the remaining 3 sts.

RIGHT SLEEVE

With US 10.5/11 (7 mm) needles and yarn held double, CO 41/45 sts. For the bottom ribbing, work in ribbing pattern for 1¼ in (3 cm) (5 rows), starting with a RS row. Begin this row with selv st, k1 and end it with k1, selv st.

Change to US 11 (8 mm) needles and continue in half brioche stitch, beginning with a WS row as shown.

At both ends of the row, BO 1 st each for the trumpet shape in the 21st and 41st row from end of cuff (37/41 sts).

After 9/8¾ in (23/22 cm) (46/44 rows) from end of cuff, mark both ends of the row. For sleeve shaping, inc 1 st each at both ends of the row for the first time in the 7th row after the marked row, then in every 6th row 5 times more (49/53 sts). Incorporate the new sts gained from the increases at both ends of the row into the half brioche stitch pattern.

After 9/8¾ in (23/22 cm) (46/44 rows) after the marked row, start raglan shaping at the left edge of the piece as follows: in the following RS row, make an accented decrease of 2 sts; then in every 4th row, accent decrease 2 sts, 5/8 times more; and in every 6th row, accent decrease 2 sts, 4/2 times more. For size 42–46 in (107–117 cm) only, in the following 4th row, BO 1 st more once by p2tog the 3rd-to-last and 4th-to-last st of the row. AT THE SAME TIME, at the right edge, for raglan shaping, make an accented decrease of 2 sts; then repeat accent decrease of 2 sts each in every 4th row, 4/8 times more; and in every 6th row, 3/0 times more. For size 42–46 in (107–117 cm) only, in the following 6th row, dec 1 st once as for the Back.

At 7½/8¼ in (38/42 rows) raglan height, BO 3 sts at the right edge for the neckline; then in every other row, BO 2 sts each 3 times more; and BO 1 st once. After the last raglan decrease, at the left edge, BO the remaining 3 sts.

FINISHING

Wet block pieces to indicated measurements and let dry.

Sew the Fronts to the Back along the side seams, making sure that the Fronts are 2 in (5 cm) shorter than the Back according to garment pattern. Sew the sleeves to the Front and Back along the raglan lines, noting the differences between right and left sleeve.

Now, work the front band separately. For this, with US 10.5/11 (7 mm) needles and yarn held double, CO 9 sts and work in ribbing pattern. After 87 in (220 cm) from cast-on row, BO all sts. Now, sew the front band to the Fronts and neckline, making sure that the middle of the band ends up at the center of the back neckline. At the bottom, sew the narrow sides of the front band to the sections of the back that extend over the Fronts so that the Fronts are now flush with the cast-on edge of the Back. Close sleeve seams.

EDGING PATTERN

Stitch count is a multiple of 2.

Row 1 (WS): Selv st (slip purlwise with yarn in back of work), k2tog-tbl, return the 2nd st of the 2 sts knit together to the left needle and knit this st together with the next st through the back loop, return the 2nd st of the 2 sts knit together to the left needle, and so on, repeating this all the way to the selv st, then return the 2nd st of the 2 sts knit together to the left needle and knit this st.

Repeat this row and work very loosely!

LINEN STITCH

Row 1 (WS): *Make a yarn over and slip 1 st purlwise, repeat from *.
Row 2 (RS): *Ssk the slipped st together with the yarn over, repeat from *.
Repeat rows 1 and 2.

PALEBEAUTY OFFBEAT LINEN STITCH VEST

DIFFICULTY LEVEL 3

SIZES

Bust circumference in oversize fit: 36–44 in (91–112 cm)

Thanks to the generous ease incorporated into the design, this vest will fit a range of sizes.

MATERIALS

- #6 super-bulky-weight yarn; shown in Lana Grossa Soffilo; 46% merino wool, 45% alpaca, 9% polyamide; 44 yd (40 m), 1.75 oz (50 g) per skein; #02 Beige, 22 skeins
- US 17.5 (15 mm) and US 36 (20 mm) knitting needles
- US P/16 (15 mm) crochet hook
- 7 buttons

GAUGE

In linen stitch on US 17.5 (15 mm) needles, 8 sts and 13 rows = 4 x 4 in (10 x 10 cm)

3-STITCH SELVEDGE

WS row: Work the first and the last 3 sts of the row as slip 1 purlwise (yarn in front of work), p1, slip 1 purlwise (yarn in front of work).
RS row: Work the first and the last 3 sts of the row as k1, slip 1 purlwise (yarn in front of work), k1.

INSTRUCTIONS

LEFT HALF OF VEST

The left half of the vest is worked in one piece from the front over the shoulder to the back, starting with the Left Front: Using US 17.5 (15 mm) needles, CO 27 sts. Begin the first row (WS) with a 3-stitch selvedge, then work 21 sts in linen stitch, and end the row with a 3-stitch selvedge.

For shaping increases at the right edge, in every other row, m1

twisted from the bar between sts after the selv st 4 times (31 sts). After 15¾ in (40 cm) (52 rows) from cast-on row, BO 6 sts once at the right edge for armhole shaping (25 sts).

From here on, work only a 1-stitch selvedge as follows: In RS rows, k the first and last st of the row. In WS rows, slip the first and last st of the row purlwise with yarn in front. After 9¾ in (25 cm) (32 rows) from the beginning of the armhole, BO sts for the neckline at the left edge: BO 6 sts once; then in every other row, BO 1 st 3 times; then BO 1 st once (14 sts).

At 3½ in (9 cm) (10 rows) from the beginning of the neckline shaping, shoulder height has been reached; now cast on sts for the back neckline at the left edge: CO 2 new sts once and in the following 2nd row, CO 9 new sts once

(25 sts). Work 1-stitch selvedge at the left edge as k1 in RS rows, as slip1 purlwise with yarn in front in WS rows.

After 13¼ in (33.5 cm) (44 rows) from shoulder line, CO 6 new sts once for armhole shaping at the right edge (31 sts). From here on, work 3-stitch selvedge at the right edge. After 13¼ in (33.5 cm) (44 rows) from the beginning of the armhole, bind off sts at the right edge: 1 st once and in every other row, BO 1 st 3 times (27 sts). After 2½ in (6.5 cm) (8 rows) from the beginning of the sloped section, BO remaining 27 sts.

RIGHT HALF OF VEST

Start at the Right Front: using US 17.5 (15 mm) needles, CO 27 sts. Begin the first row (WS) with 3-stitch selvedge, then work 21 sts in linen stitch and end the row with a 3-stitch selvedge.

For shaping increases at the left edge, in every other row, m1 twisted from the bar between sts before the selv st 4 times (31 sts). After 15¾ in (40 cm) (52 rows) from cast-on row, BO 6 sts once at the left edge for armhole shaping (25 sts).

From here on, work only a 1-stitch selvedge as follows: In RS

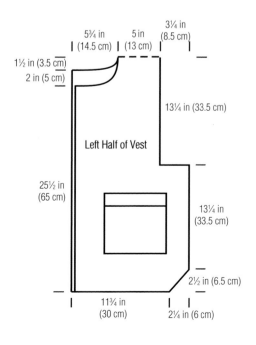

5¾ in (14.5 cm) 5 in (13 cm) 3¼ in (8.5 cm)

1½ in (3.5 cm)
2 in (5 cm)

13¼ in (33.5 cm)

Left Half of Vest

25½ in (65 cm)

13¼ in (33.5 cm)

2½ in (6.5 cm)

11¾ in (30 cm)   2¼ in (6 cm)

rows, k the first and last st of the row. In WS rows, slip the first and last st of the row purlwise with yarn in front. After 9¾ in (25 cm) (32 rows) from the beginning of the armhole, BO sts for the neckline at the right edge: BO 6 sts once; then in every other row, BO 1 st 3 times; then BO 1 st once (14 sts).

At 3½ in (9 cm) (10 rows) from the beginning of the neckline shaping, shoulder height has been reached; now cast on sts for the back neckline at the right edge: CO 2 new sts once and in the following 2nd row, CO 9 new sts once (25 sts). Work 1-stitch selvedge at the right edge as k1 in RS rows, as slip1 purlwise with yarn in front in WS rows.

After 13¼ in (33.5 cm) (44 rows) from shoulder line, CO 6 new sts once for armhole shaping at the left edge (31 sts). From here on, work 3-stitch selvedge at the left edge. After 13¼ in (33.5 cm) (44 rows) from the beginning of the armhole, bind off sts at the left edge: 1 st once and in every other row, BO 1 st 3 times (27 sts). After 2½ in (6.5 cm) (8 rows) from the beginning of the sloped section, BO remaining 27 sts.

POCKET

Using US 17.5 (15 mm) needles, CO 9 sts. Work 1-stitch selvedge and linen stitch in between. For side extensions, m1 twisted at both ends of the row (before/after the selv st) in every other row 2 times (13 sts).

After 6½ in (17 cm) (20 rows) from cast-on row, change to US 36 (20 mm) needles and continue in edging pattern, increasing 1 st in the first row (14 sts). Work edging pattern very loosely. After 2¼ in (6 cm) (5 rows) in edging pattern, BO all sts with crocheted slip stitch.

Work the other pocket the same way.

FINISHING

Wet block pieces to indicated measurements and let dry.

Sew the pockets to the Fronts 4 in (10 cm) from the front edge and 4¾ in (12 cm) from the bottom edge of the vest.

Close the back seam.

Using US 17.5 (15 mm) needles, pick up and knit 58 sts along the neckline edge and work in edging pattern for 2¼ in (6 cm) (5 rows), working 3-stitch selvedge over first and last 3 sts of the row. Here, too, BO with 1 row of crocheted slip stitch.

With US 17.5 (15 mm) needles, pick up and knit 42 sts each from the vertical armhole edges, then work in edging pattern for 2¼ in (6 cm) (5 rows). Here, too, BO with 1 row of crocheted slip stitch.

Sew on the narrow sides of the front bands. At the sides, sew 3 buttons each to the straight part of the Fronts between the beginning of the armhole and bottom curve. Attach another button to the Left Front below the neckband. Button by using the gaps between sts as buttonholes.

STOCKINETTE STITCH
Knit on RS, purl on WS.

ACCENTED INCREASES
In WS rows, make a yarn over. In the following RS row, knit this yarn over through the back loop.

ACCENTED DECREASES A
Decreasing 1 st: At the beginning of the row, after the first two sts, work sl1, k1, psso. At the end of the row, work to last 4 sts, then knit the 3rd and 4th-to-last sts together, work 2 selv sts.

Decreasing 2 sts: At the beginning of the row, after the first two sts, work sl1, k2tog, psso. At the end of the row, work to last 5 sts, k3tog the 5th-, 4th- and 3rd-to-last sts, work 2 selv sts.

ACCENTED DECREASES B
Decreasing 1 st: At the beginning of the row, after the selv st, work sl1, k1, psso. At the end of the row, work to last 3 sts, k2tog, selv st.

Decreasing 2 sts: At the beginning of the row, after the selv st, sl1, k2tog, psso (slip 1 knitwise, knit the following 2 sts together and pass the slipped st over). At the end of the row, work to last 4 sts, k3tog, selv st.

COLOR SEQUENCE A FOR BACK AND FRONT
15 rows with A held double
10 rows with 1 strand each of A and B held together
12 rows with B held double
14 rows with 1 strand each of B and C held together
Rest of the rows in C held double

ROSEWOOD SUMMER SWEATER IN COTTON AND SILK

DIFFICULTY LEVEL 1

SIZES
Bust circumference for oversize fit: 36–40/42–46 in (91–102/107–117 cm)

Numbers for size 36–40 in (91–102 cm) are listed before the slash, for size 42–46 in (107–117 cm) after the slash. If only one number is given, it applies to both sizes.

MATERIALS
- #4 medium-weight yarn; shown in Lana Grossa California; 80% cotton, 20% silk; 120 yd (110 m), 1.75 oz (50 g) per skein; 6/7 skeins #017 Plum (A), 4 skeins each in #303 Antique Pink Rosewood (B) and #016 Rosé (C)
- US 11 (8 mm) and US 17 (12 mm) knitting needles
- US 11 (8 mm) circular knitting needle, 24 in (60 cm) long

GAUGE
In stockinette stitch on US 17 (12 mm) needles with yarn held double, 10.5 sts and 10 rows (measured hanging) = 4 x 4 in (10 x 10 cm)

COLOR SEQUENCE B FOR SLEEVES

11 rows with A held double

10 rows with 1 strand each of A and B held together

12 rows with B held double

14 rows with 1 strand each of B and C held together

Rest of the rows in C held double

INSTRUCTIONS

BACK

With US 11 (8 mm) needles and A held double, CO 58/62 sts and work for 2 in (5 cm) (9 rows) in stockinette stitch.

Change to US 17 (12 mm) needles and continue in stockinette stitch, starting with color sequence A. In row 16 (WS) from needle size change, make an accented increase of 1 st each before and after the middle 18 sts. Rep accent increase of 1 st each before the

first and after the last increased st in every 4th row, 4 times more; then in every other row, 6 times more. To even out, work accented decrease A of 1 st each at both side edges first in row 17; then repeat accent decrease of 1 st each in every 4th row, 4 times more; then in every other row, 6 times more. This way, the stitch count between the increases always increases by 2 and the stitch count to the side edge accordingly decreases by 1 st each, while the overall stitch count stays unchanged (58/62 sts).

After 18 in (46 cm) (46 rows) from needle size change, work accented decrease A of 2 sts each at both ends of the row for armhole shaping, then in every other row, accented decrease A of 1 st each, 5 times more (44/48 sts).

When armhole has reached a depth of 8/8¾ in (20/22 cm) (20/22 rows), BO 5/6 sts each

for shoulder sloping at both ends of the row at the beginning of the next RS and WS rows; then at the beginning of the following RS and WS rows, BO 4/5 sts each once. AT THE SAME TIME as the first shoulder shaping decrease, for the round neckline, before and after the middle 20 sts, work accent decrease of 2 sts each; and between these decreases, BO the middle 20 sts, then continue both parts separately. For further neckline shaping, at the inside (neck) edge, in the 2nd row, work accented decrease B of 1 st. With this, the sts on one side have been used up. Finish the other side the same way, but mirror inverted.

FRONT

With US 11 (8 mm) needles and A held double, CO 58/62 sts and work for 2 in (5 cm) (9 rows) in stockinette stitch.

Change to US 17 (12 mm) needles and continue in stockinette stitch, starting with color sequence A. In row 16 (WS) from needle size change, make an accented increase of 1 st each before and after the middle 18 sts. Repeat accent increase of 1 st each before the first and after the last increased st in every 4th row, 4 times more; then in every other row, 6 times more. To even out, work accented decrease A of 1 st each at both side edges first in row 17; then repeat accent decrease of 1 st each in every 4th row, 4 times more; then in every other row, 6 times more. This way, the stitch count between the increases always increases by 2 and the stitch count to the side

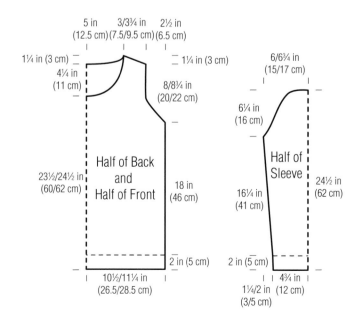

(continued) ROSEWOOD

edge accordingly decreases by 1 st each, while the overall stitch count stays unchanged (58/62 sts).

After 18 in (46 cm) (46 rows) from needle size change, work accented decrease A of 2 sts each at both ends of the row for armhole shaping; then in every other row, accented decrease A of 1 st each, 5 times more (44/48 sts).

When armhole has reached a depth of 3½/4¼ in (9/11 cm) (9/11 rows), BO the middle 16 sts and continue both parts separately. For further neckline shaping, at the inside (neck) edge, in every other row, work accented decrease B of 1 st each, 5 times more.

When armhole has reached a depth of 8/8¾ in (20/22 cm) (20/22 rows), BO 5/6 sts each for shoulder sloping at the right/left

edge of the piece once; then in the 2nd row, BO 4/5 sts each once.

SLEEVES

With US 11 (8 mm) needles and A held double, CO 28 sts, then work in stockinette stitch, beginning with a WS row in purl.

When piece has reached a height of 2 in (5 cm) (9 rows) from cast-on row, change to US 17 (12 mm) needles and continue in stockinette, starting with color sequence B. For sleeve shaping, make increases at both ends of the row in row 11/row 3 from needle size change after the 2nd st and before the last 2 sts of the row: m1 twisted each from the bar between sts, then inc 1 st each the same way in every 10th/8th row, 2/4 times more (34/38 sts).

After 16¼ in (41 cm) (42 rows) from needle size change, work accented decrease A of 2 sts each at both ends of the row for the sleeve cap; then repeat accent decrease in every other row, 2 sts each, 0/1 time(s); 1 st each, 6/4 times; 2 sts each, 1/2 time(s). In the following row, BO the remaining 14 sts.

Work the other sleeve the same way.

FINISHING

Wet block pieces to indicated measurements and let dry.

Sew Front and Back together at the shoulders and sides. Close sleeve seams.

With US 11 (8 mm) circular needle and yarn B held double, pick up and knit 70 sts around the neckline edge. For the neckline, knit for 6 rnds, then BO sts.

Sew the sleeves into the armholes.

》》》 This construction makes the middle parts of the Front and Back pull a little bit upward while the sides are slightly longer because of slack.

REFERENCES
CHARTS AND TECHNIQUES

CHARTS

SunDowner
Page 64

Chart A

Chart B

- ■ = knit 1
- – = purl 1
- ☐ = no stitch, for better overview only
- + = increase 1 knitwise from the bar between sts
- ✕ = increase 1 purlwise from the bar between sts

■■■■/– = hold 1 st on cable needle behind work, knit the next 4 sts, then purl 1 from cable needle

–\■■■■ = hold 4 sts on cable needle in front of work, purl the next st, then knit the 4 sts from the cable needle

■■■■/■■■■ = hold 4 sts on cable needle behind work, knit the next 4 sts, then knit the 4 sts from the cable needle

■■■■\■■■■ = hold 4 sts on cable needle in front of work, knit the next 4 sts, then knit the 4 sts from the cable needle

SandDunes

Page 85

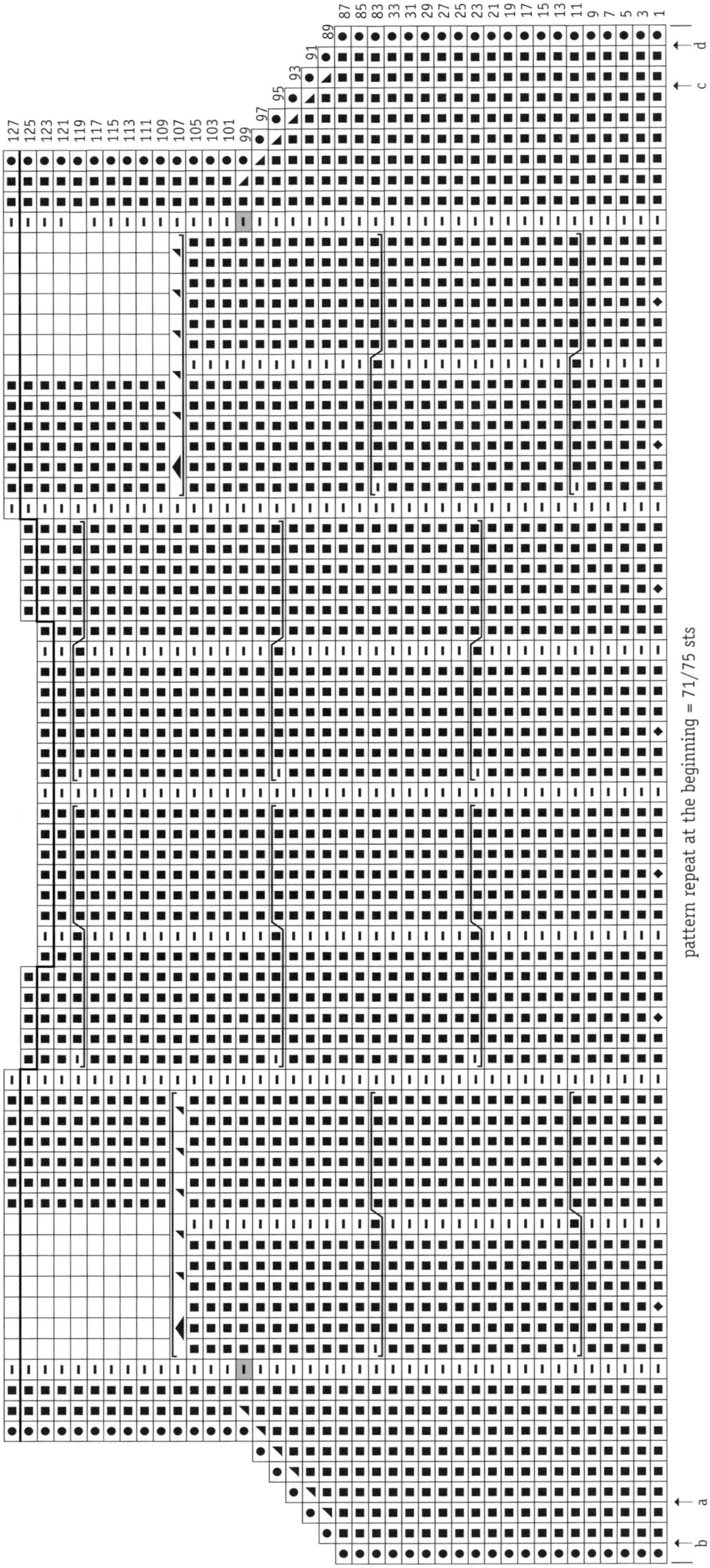
pattern repeat at the beginning = 71/75 sts

Chart B

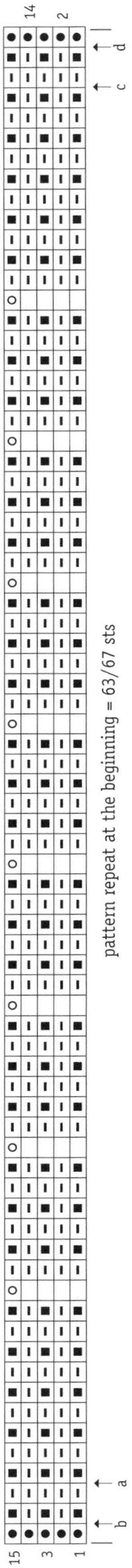
pattern repeat at the beginning = 63/67 sts

Chart A

Sand**Dunes**

Page 85

Chart D

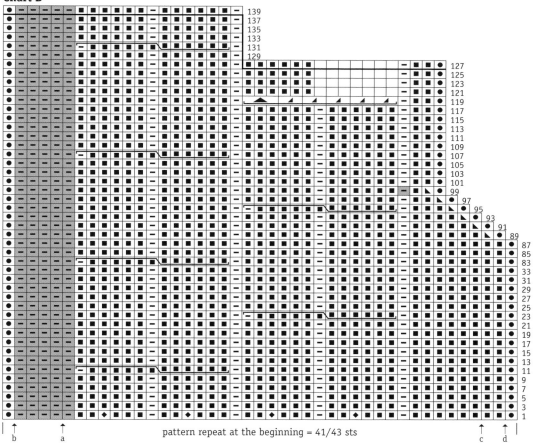

pattern repeat at the beginning = 41/43 sts

b   a

c   d

Chart C

pattern repeat = 37/39 sts

b   c   d

Key: see page 107

SandDunes

Page 85

Chart F

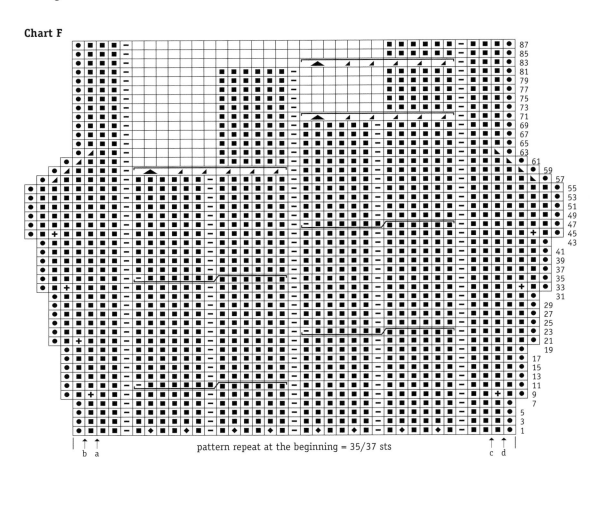

b a   pattern repeat at the beginning = 35/37 sts   c d

Charts E und G

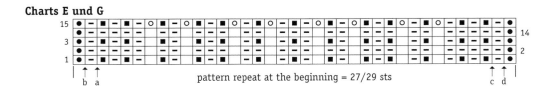

b a   pattern repeat at the beginning = 27/29 sts   c d

SandDunes
Page 85

Chart H

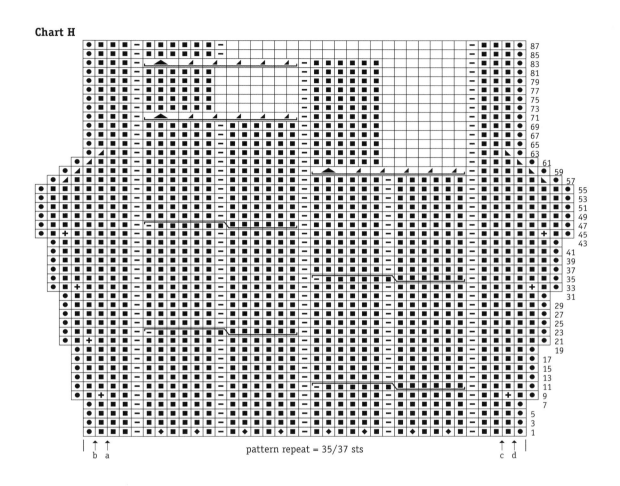

pattern repeat = 35/37 sts

b a

c d

● = 1 selvedge stitch

■ = knit 1 on RS and WS

– = purl 1 on RS and WS

☐ = no stitch, for better overview only

◢ = knit 2 sts together

◣ = slip 1 knitwise, knit next st, pass slipped st over

○ = 1 yarn over

◆ = knit 1 through the back loop

✚ = increase 1 knitwise from the bar between sts

= hold 6 sts on cable needle behind work, knit 6, purl 1, then knit the 6 sts from the cable needle

= hold 6 sts on cable needle in front of work, knit 6, purl 1, then knit the 6 sts from the cable needle

= hold 6 sts on cable needle behind work, then (k2tog 1 st from the left needle with 1 st from the cable needle) 5 times in all, k3tog the last 2 sts from the left needle with the last st from the cable needle

= hold 6 sts on cable needle in front of work, then (k2tog 1 st from the left needle with 1 st from the cable needle) 5 times in all, k3tog the last st from the cable needle with the last 2 sts from the left needle

TECHNIQUES

JOINING PIECES WITH MATTRESS STITCH

FIRST JOIN (FIGURE 8)

1. Place the two pieces to be joined next to each other right side up so their edges meet. Join the selvedge stitches from the bottom (cast-on) edge of both pieces in a figure 8 motion by going through both pieces, inserting the tapestry needle directly above the cast-on edge from the back to the front and from the bottom up, exiting before the selvedge stitch of the left piece, from the bottom up, exiting before the selvedge stitch of the right piece, then pulling the yarn through. Leave an end of at least 6 in (15 cm) to be woven in later.

2. Again from the bottom up, exit a second time in the same spot, first on the left piece, then on the right piece, then tighten the yarn properly.

JOINING STOCKINETTE STITCH FABRIC

Mattress stitch can be worked much faster on pieces worked in stockinette than on those in other stitch patterns because two bars in subsequent rows can be grasped at the same time.

1. To prepare for seaming, first insert the tapestry needle into the previous exit spot of the right piece, lead the needle along the column of bars, grasp the next bar above the exit spot, and pull the working yarn through.

2. Insert the tapestry needle into the previous exit spot of the left piece, lead the needle along the column of bars, grasp the next two bars above the exit spot, and pull the working yarn through.

3. Insert the tapestry needle into the previous exit spot of the right piece, lead the needle along the column of bars, grasp the next two bars above the exit spot, and pull the working yarn through.

Repeat Steps 2 and 3, always joining the left and the right piece over a section the height of 2 bars. Pull the working yarn tight so that the knitted pieces get pulled together until the outmost pattern stitches (after the selvedge stitch) meet, and the seam on the right side of the fabric blends in with the stockinette stitches. The seam has the correct tension if it stays invisible even when the two knitted pieces are pulled apart slightly. Pulling the working yarn too hard, however, will cause the seam to become too tight and the knitted fabric to bunch up.

JOINING GARTER STITCH FABRIC

To join two garter stitch pieces, the selvedge stitches have to be worked in garter stitch as well.

First, join both bottom selvedge stitches in a figure 8 form. After this, alternating between right and left pieces, always pick up one bar from the first garter stitch ridge above the exit spot, and pull the working yarn through.

JOINING TWO CAST-ON OR BIND-OFF EDGES

When connecting either two adjoining cast-on of bind-off edges, the knitting direction of the stitches will be reversed after pieces have been seamed. For an even stitch definition at the transition from the seam to the stitches after it, work the mattress stitch seam shifted by half a stitch.

1. Place the two pieces to be joined next to each other right side up so their edges meet. Join the right edges of both pieces in a figure 8 form one row in from the cast-on or bind-off row between the selvedge stitch and the first pattern stitch as follows: Exit the tapestry needle from the bottom up out of the center of the selvedge stitch out of the right piece, exit from the bottom up after the selvedge stitch of the left piece, and pull the working yarn through. Leave an end of at least 6 in (15 cm) to be woven in later. Once again, exit from the bottom up out of the center of the selvedge stitch out of the right piece, from the bottom up after the selvedge stitch of the left piece, and pull the working yarn through tightly.

2. Alternatingly, with your tapestry needle, pick up both legs of the following stitches of the left and right pieces. For the right piece, insert the needle into the center of the stitch, grasping both legs of 2 sts at once, while for the left piece, grasping both legs of only one stitch.

JOINING A SIDE EDGE TO A CAST-ON OR BIND-OFF EDGE

For most stitch patterns, 4 rows in height equal about 3 sts in width. This rule of thumb will be sufficient in most cases to achieve a flat but still stretchy seam. For seaming in mattress stitch, the 3 out of 4 rule means that 3 sts have always to be joined to 4 rows. Straight seams can be closed the same way without having to preliminary baste them.

The easiest way to produce this seam is to always join both legs of a stitch to one bar between stitches in mattress stitch, skipping every 4th bar in the process.

PICKING UP STITCHES

FROM A BIND-OFF ROW

1. Insert your knitting needle from front to back into the stitch below the bind-off edge. Make sure to insert your needle into the center of each stitch, not in the void between stitches!

2. Grasp the working yarn and pull it through.

FROM A CAST-ON ROW

In order for the new stitches to blend in with the existing ones, insert needle between existing stitches and shift the new row of stitches by half a stitch. At the right and left edge of the piece, half a stitch is lost this way, so when working in rows, one additional stitch has to be picked up out of the center of the last selvedge stitch for adjustment.

FROM A SIDE EDGE

When picking up stitches from a side edge, the newly picked up stitches will be aligned sideways to the stitches of the existing knitted piece. For this reason, the 3 out of 4 rule also applies here: if 3 sts are as wide as 4 rows are high, stitches are picked up in groups of three, skipping every 4th row.

WORKING HALF BRIOCHE STITCH (FISHERMAN'S RIB)

KNITTED BRIOCHE STITCH

1. In a WS row, place the working yarn in front of the work and slip the stitch (which, on this side of the fabric, looks like a purl stitch) purlwise, wrapping the working yarn from front to back over the right needle to create a yarn over.

2. In the following RS row, insert the right needle knitwise into the stitch (on this side of the fabric, looking like a knit stitch) and knit the stitch together with the yarn over.

PURLED BRIOCHE STITCH

1. In a RS row, place the working yarn in front of the work and slip the stitch (on this side of the fabric, looking like a knit stitch) purlwise, wrapping the working yarn from front to back over the right needle to create a yarn over.

2. In the following WS row, insert the right needle purlwise into the stitch (on this side of the fabric, looking like a purl stitch) and purl the stitch together with the yarn over.

CASTING ON ADDITIONAL STITCHES

If multiple stitches need to be added to a knitted piece at once, they can be created using the backwards loop cast-on method. Using the backwards loop cast-on, as many new stitches as needed are added on one after another. With this method, new stitches can be added to the left edge of the knitted piece from right to left using the working yarn.

New stitches will sit on the needle twisted, with the left leg of the stitch sitting in front of the needle and the right leg of the stitch sitting behind the needle. After the next row has been worked, these stitches are twisted in the knitted fabric, even though they need to be worked like regular stockinette stitches.

1. To wind on a base loop, hold the tail end of the working yarn with the middle, ring, and pinkie finger of your left hand. The right hand holds the knitting needle and the end of the working yarn that's attached to the skein. Raise the left thumb. With your right hand, place the working yarn clockwise and from the outside inward around the left thumb and cross it over the yarn tail in front of the thumb. Insert the right needle underneath the yarn in front of the thumb.

2. With the needle, lift the loop from the thumb and pull the yarn tight in the direction of the needle. Hold onto both strands until casting on the next loop.

CROCHET STITCHES

SINGLE CROCHET

1. Insert your crochet hook as if to pick up and knit stitches, place the working yarn onto the left index finger and leave a tail of about 8 in (20 cm) to be woven in later. Move the crochet hook in a clockwise direction around the working yarn, grasp the working yarn, and pull it through. Grasp the working yarn once more above the edge of the knitted piece and pull it through the crocheted loop.

2. Insert hook into next stitch and grasp the working yarn and pull it through. Grasp the working yarn again and pull it through both loops on the hook. Repeat the last step until you have crocheted over the entire length of the knitted piece.

REVERSE SINGLE CROCHET (CRAB STITCH)

For reverse single crochet (crab stitch) edging, the single crochets for the 2nd row are not worked on the wrong side, but still on the right side of the fabric, without turning, and from left to right. After 1 row of single crochets has been worked around the edge of the knitted piece, continue without turning in the opposite direction for one row.

Crochet a chain into the last stitch of the first crocheted row: For this, grasp the working yarn with the crochet hook and pull it through the loop. Now, insert the crochet hook into the next whole stitch—that is, under both loops of the stitch to the right of the first stitch, grasp the working yarn and pull it through. Grasp the working yarn again over the

knitted edge, and now, pull it through both crocheted loops. For the next crab stitch, insert hook again into the next whole stitch to the right of the stitch last worked, and work another single crochet stitch.

BINDING OFF IN SLIP STITCH

1. Insert crochet hook into the first stitch as if to knit and pull the working yarn through. *Insert the crochet hook knitwise into the next stitch on the left needle and grasp the working yarn.

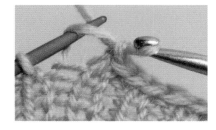

2. Now, pull the working yarn through both the stitch on the left needle and the loop on the crochet hook at once. Repeat from *.

Salt 'n' Pepper
Page 20

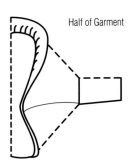

>>> Arrows in the schematic indicate the knitting direction.

Half of Garment

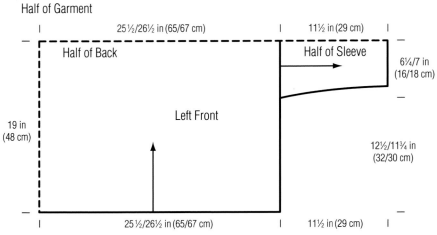

Half of Garment

Half of Back

25½/26½ in (65/67 cm)

11½ in (29 cm)

Half of Sleeve

6¼/7 in (16/18 cm)

Left Front

19 in (48 cm)

12½/11¾ in (32/30 cm)

25½/26½ in (65/67 cm)

11½ in (29 cm)

ABBREVIATIONS

BO = bind off

cm = centimeter

CO = cast on

g = grams

in = inch(es)

inc = increase

k = knit

k2tog = knit 2 sts together

k3tog = knit 3 sts together

m1 = make 1 from the bar
    between sts

oz = ounces

p = purl

p2tog = purl 2 sts together

rep = repeat

rnd(s) = round(s)

RS = right side (row)

selv st = selvedge stitch(es)

sl1, k1, psso = slip 1 knitwise, knit
    one, pass slipped stitch over

sl1, k2tog, psso = slip 1, knit the
    next 2 sts together, pass slipped
    stitch over

ssk = slip, slip, knit

ssp = slip, slip, purl

st(s) = stitch(es)

tbl = through back of loop

WS = wrong side (row)

yd = yards

yo = yarn over(s)